# Economic Transformation in Russia

# Economic Transformation in Russia

**Edited by ANDERS ÅSLUND**

PINTER
PUBLISHERS
LONDON

**Pinter Publishers Ltd**
25 Floral Street, Covent Garden
London WC2E 9DS, United Kingdom

First published in 1994



**British Library Cataloguing in Publication Data**
A CIP record for this book is available from the British Library

ISBN 1 85567 199 9
1 85567 302 9 (pbk)



Set in Monotype Ehrhardt by Ewan Smith
48 Shacklewell Lane, London E8 2EY

Printed in Great Britain by SRP Ltd., Exeter

# Contents

# List of Contributors

*Anders Åslund* Professor, Director, Stockholm Institute of East European Economics, Stockholm School of Economics; Economic Advisor to the Russian Government, and Co-Director of the Macroeconomic and Finance Unit (MFU) of the Russian Government.

*Petr Aven* Dr., Research Fellow IIASA, Laxenburg; President of Alfa Bank; Minister of External Economic Relations of the Russian Federation, November 1991–December 1992.

*Irina Boeva* Dr., Research Fellow, Working Center for Economic Reform, Government of the Russian Federation.

*Maxim Boycko* Dr., Economic Advisor, State Committee for State Property Management of the Russian Federation (GKI).

*Anatoly B. Chubais* Dr., Deputy Prime Minister, Chairman of the State Committee for State Property Management of the Russian Federation (GKI).

*Tatiana Dolgopiatova* Dr., Research Fellow, Institute of the Economic Problems of the Transition Period, Moscow.

*Boris G. Fedorov* Professor, Deputy Prime Minister, Minister of Finance of the Russian Federation.

*Stanley Fischer* Professor of Economics, Department of Economics, MIT; Research Associate, NBER.

*Andrei N. Illarionov* Dr., Chief Economic Advisor to the Prime Minister and Deputy Director, Working Center for Economic Reform, Government of the Russian Federation.

*Andrei I. Kazmin* Dr., Deputy Minister of Finance of the Russian Federation.

*Richard Layard* Professor of Economics, Director of the Centre for Economic Performance, London School of Economics.

*Vitaly A. Naishul* Director, Institute for the Study of the Russian Economy, Moscow.

*Peter Orszag* Staff Economist, Council of Economic Advisors, Executive Office of the President, US Government.

*Jacek Rostowski* School of Slavonic and East European Studies, University of London, Centre for Research into Communist Economics, Centre for Economic Performance.

*Jeffrey D. Sachs* Galen L. Stone Professor of International Trade, Harvard University, Economic Advisor to the Russian Government, and Co-Director of the Macroeconomic and Finance Unit (MFU) of the Russian Government.

*Andrei Shleifer* Professor of Economics, Harvard University; Economic Advisor, State Committee for State Property Management of Russia.

*Maria Vishnevskaya* Research Fellow, International Center for Economic Transformation, Moscow.

*Robert W. Vishny* Dr., Professor of Economics, University of Chicago.

# Acknowledgements

On 14–15 June 1993, the Stockholm Institute of East European Economics held a conference at the Stockholm School of Economics on Economic Transformation in Russia. It was the third conference of its kind, attracting economists preoccupied with the change of economic system in Russia both from Russia and elsewhere. The papers included in this book were commissioned for and presented at that conference. After a lively discussion, the papers have been revised by the authors. I would like to express my gratitude to the authors of the papers included, and to the the active participants in the conference.

The conference and the book are based on the ongoing collaboration between reformers in the Government of the Russian Federation and a variety of Western economists. The basis of the whole undertaking is the openness of the Russian Government, and its desire to form a market economic system. Its manifold assistance is keenly appreciated. Members of the Macroeconomic and Finance Unit of the Russian Government have contributed much of the underlying research.

The conference was prepared by the staff of Stockholm Institute of East European Economics. Marion Cutting has provided extensive and vital editorial assistance, checked the language and administered the editorial process. Gun Malmquist has kindly provided excellent secretarial services.

The conference was generously financed by the Ministry of Foreign Affairs of Sweden. The work of the Macroeconomic and Finance Unit of the Russian Government has been financed by the Government of Sweden and the Ford Foundation. Their support is gratefully acknowledged. Finally, I want to express my great appreciation of Dr Frances Pinter and her excellent and always so friendly staff.

Notwithstanding the numerous people who have kindly contributed to the production of this book, the ultimate responsibility for any remaining errors must fall upon its editor.

*Anders Åslund*
*Stockholm and Moscow, October 1993*

# Introduction

A fundamental change of economic system has been going on in Russia for almost two years. The milestone remains the programmatic speech by Russia's President Boris Yeltsin on 28 October 1991, when the Soviet Union still lingered on. His declaration was swiftly followed by the appointment of a reform-oriented government with a number of young bright economists, whose leader was and remains Yegor Gaidar. Other members of his team were Deputy Prime Minister Alexander Shokhin, Minister of Privatization Anatoly Chubais, and Minister for External Economic Relations Petr Aven. At the beginning of 1992, a major liberalization occurred, accompanied by both an attempt at macroeconomic stabilization and extensive privatization.

In political terms, Russia seems peculiar in comparison with successful transitional economies in Eastern Europe. Countries such as Poland, Czechia, Slovakia, Hungary, Slovenia, Estonia and Latvia have all undergone full democratization, including new parliamentary elections, and they have elected non-communist governments which have undertaken a fundamental transformation of the economic system into a market economy. Russia has also had a non-communist government that has opted for a full transition to a market economy, but the political base for this policy has been lacking.

So far, the Russian transition has been characterized by an uneasy balance between the government's ambitious attempts to profoundly alter the economic system and the political opposition of the recalcitrant, pre-democratic parliament. After the abortive coup of August 1991, it briefly seemed that the communist opposition to market economy, private ownership and the rule of law was broken for good. At the time, few argued for early elections to the not-so-democratically elected Congress of People's Deputies, which within itself elected the Supreme Soviet. In hindsight, as the President himself has stated, his biggest mistake was not calling for new parliamentary elections immediately after the failed August 1991 coup. At that time, the Congress of People's Deputies might have concurred with his proposal, and according to the old Soviet Russian constitution of 1978, the parliament was sovereign. With two-thirds' majority, the Congress of People's Deputies could instantly change the constitution at whim.

The deputies have evidenced a stunning capacity for flexibility and political transformation. When they were elected in the spring of 1990, 87 per cent were members of the Communist Party, though for many this membership was little but an expedient for their careers. Increasingly, the deputies moved in a liberal and democratic direction, but this process peaked in August 1991, and a reversal started. As various deputies found that their careers as 'democrats' were not sufficiently successful, they switched their stance and opted for other political groups that were prepared to offer them higher posts, or they simply returned to their prior political opinions. During the first half of 1992, President Yeltsin could still on occasion sway the Congress of People's Deputies to support him, but after June 1992 its majority opposed him firmly, and it grew ever stronger and more militant.

It is against this political background the economic transformation must be seen. The golden window of opportunity of the reform government lasted from November 1991 until April 1992, when a session of the Congress of People's Deputies made evident how strong its resistance to market economic reforms really was, even if the opposition formulated it in other terms. The reformers managed to undertake a far-reaching liberalization during that period, introduce a reasonably balanced budget, and monetary policy was relatively strict until June 1992.

During the second quarter of 1992, the reformers gradually lost their grip. Even so, at the last possible opportunity, Deputy Prime Minister Anatoly Chubais succeeded in getting the Supreme Soviet to adopt his Privatization Programme and Law on Privatization. A stable foundation for his privatization process had been laid.

In the second half of 1992, the parliament's opposition to the government and the President grew ever stronger. Yegor Gaidar, who had become acting Prime Minister in the summer, came increasingly under attack. In December 1992, the Congress of People's Deputies finally managed to oust him, and he was replaced by a middle-aged technocrat and industrialist, Viktor Chernomyrdin. At the same time, Gaidar's ally Petr Aven was ousted as Minister for External Economic Relations. In the meantime, macroeconomic policy disintegrated altogether amidst a massive credit expansion in the third quarter of 1992, when the former Chairman of the old Soviet State Bank Viktor Gerashchenko was appointed as Chairman of the Central Bank of Russia in July 1992. The Central Bank was subservient to the Parliament, and Gerashchenko was sensitive to its demands for monetary expansion and industrial policy through subsidized direct credits. Nor was any further liberalization possible during the second half of 1992. Curiously, privatization continued at full speed, virtually unabated in spite of the political stalemate. The Supreme Soviet opposed Chubais's privatization policies, but they had already adopted the key decisions, and Chubais proceeded on the basis of presidential and governmental decrees.

In December 1992, it looked as if the whole economic transition would fall victim to the hostile Congress of People's Deputies, but Chubais and Shokhin managed to stay on in government, and another young liberal economist, Boris Fedorov, was appointed Deputy Prime Minister and Minister of Finance. At the time, Russia was on the verge of hyperinflation because of a massive monetary expansion from June to October 1992. However, with the establishment of a Government Credit Committee in October 1992, Gaidar had managed to impede the expansion of credits in November 1992. Inflation peaked in January 1993 at 27 per cent per month and started slowly declining under the impact of the extraordinary efforts at macroeconomic stabilization by Boris Fedorov despite massive opposition from the parliament, the Central Bank and several members of the Government. In parallel, the voucher privatization of large and medium-sized enterprises took off.

The year of 1993 has been characterized by political cycles. In March, the conflict between the President and the Congress of People's Deputies rose to a crescendo. A referendum was finally agreed between the two parties for 25 April. Apart from a vote of confidence for the President, the referendum included a question on support for the economic policies of the President and the Government initiated in 1992. As most had expected, the President won the vote of confidence, with a comfortable majority of 59 per cent, but it came as a surprise to most that no less than 53 per cent of the votes cast were positive to the economic policies. The referendum gave a reformist impetus that lasted for almost three months, but this did little more than balance out the prior communist offensive. From mid-July until mid-September, a new conservative offensive launched by the parliament, the Central Bank and conservative members of the government followed. The government itself was badly stifled by a conflict in its midst over all fundamental principles of economic policy, primarily between Boris Fedorov and the new conservative First Deputy Prime Minister and Minister of Economy Oleg Lobov, who had been appointed in April 1993 in anticipation of a negative vote on the Government's economic policies.

Finally, in mid-September 1993 Prime Minister Chernomyrdin and President Yeltsin decided to remove Lobov from the Government, and Yegor Gaidar agreed to take his place as First Deputy Prime Minister and Minister of Economy. A few days later, on 21 September, President Yeltsin dissolved the Congress of People's Deputies and the Supreme Soviet by decree and called for elections to a new parliament on 12 December. The old parliament disqualified itself in the public eye through its violent uprising of 3–4 October.

When he re-entered the Government, Gaidar immediately tipped the balance within the Government towards fundamental economic transformation. A programme of liberalization, macroeconomic stabilization and various structural changes was swiftly drawn up. Again, the principles were truly market-oriented. Many important changes have already been undertaken, but a real macroeconomic stabilization is not likely to occur until parliamentary elections have been won by liberal forces. If the liberal parties win the elections in December, a unique opportunity for a more successful attempt at building a market economy and combating inflation would open up.

It is in this political and economic context the eleven papers of this book should be seen. They were originally written in the aftermath of the April referendum, when optimism prevailed. The mood of the current pre-election campaign is rather similar. On the one hand, more time has passed without convincing success, especially in the combat of inflation. On the other hand, no catastrophe has occurred, and now the old parliament is finally dissolved. New truly democratic parliamentary elections are about to be held for the first time. Optimistic and pessimistic moods alternate, but actual developments tend to be neither as bad as one feared, nor as good as one hoped.

This book is the third of its kind. It is the result of collaboration of the reformist members of the Russian Government and their domestic and foreign advisers, though the advisers speak for themselves and not for the Russian Government. Although there are significant differences in the views of the contributors, they all belong to the current of thought supporting the attempts at economic transformation by the present Russian Government. Two of the authors, Boris Fedorov and Anatoly Chubais, serve as Deputy Prime Ministers, while Petr Aven has left the Government. All the contributors are also academics, but several of the chapters are strongly policy-oriented. Our hope is that this volume will provide the reader with an analytical picture of the current state of the Russian economy, of achievements and failures to date, and of the line of thinking that is underlying the policies of the Russian Government.

The first four papers of the book deal with macroeconomic themes. *Stanley Fischer* provides an overview of the prospects for financial and monetary stabilization and reviews the Government's attempt at stabilization. His conclusion is that stabilization is within reach, and he outlines what measures the Government needs to undertake to accomplish it, as well as clarifying the role of international financial support.

Deputy Prime Minister and Minister of Finance *Boris Fedorov* and Deputy Minister of Finance *Andrei Kazmin* review their experiences of attempts at financial and monetary stabilization in 1993. They try to explain why the stabilization attempts failed in the third quarter of 1993, and what future consequences this failure will have. Their conclusion, however, is that the situation and economic policy have become more predictable and manageable. Even if credit ceilings were exceeded in the third quarter of 1993, monetary expansion was only one-third of its volume in the third quarter of 1992.

*Jeffrey D. Sachs* presents his view of the prospects for monetary stabilization in Russia in a very substantial paper. Economically, he sees ample opportunities, which he specifies. But in his view, the biggest obstacle is the political will of the executive branch of the state to stand behind a rigorous stabilization programme. The foremost economic measure that is required for stabilization is to put an end to the ruble area.

If stabilization is achieved, a number of other monetary and financial problems would arise, as Eastern Europe's experience has shown. *Jacek Rostowski* looks into several of these issues, such as the behaviour of the money supply after stabilization, the choice of exchange rate, bad debts in the banking sector and inter-enterprise debts. If these problems are not properly handled, a financial crisis can easily follow on the heels of an inflation crisis.

In a forceful account of the problems in foreign trade regulation, *Petr Aven* sums up his various insights from his experiences as Minister for External Economic Relations during the first year of serious economic transformation in Russia. He draws rather diverse conclusions, but one major lesson is that any obstacle to economic activity, especially if it involves a discretionary choice, will be circumvented in Russia, which is an argument for a particularly liberal regime in Russia.

Deputy Prime Minister and Minister for Privatization *Anatoly Chubais* together with researcher *Maria Vishnevskaya* has provided an overview of privatization, and

*Maxim Boycko*, *Andrei Shleifer* and *Robert W. Vishny* offer an account of the progress of Russian privatization. Both papers focus on various aspects of the voucher privatization of large-scale enterprises, which at present appears to be a stunning success with a fast transfer of tens of millions of shares into the hands of private Russian citizens. And this privatization even seems to be accelerating. Restructuring, however, has barely started, and it is too early to pass any judgement on how successful this will be in Russia.

*Irina Boeva* and *Tatiana Dolgopiatova* have undertaken interviews at ten state enterprises to see how they are forming strategies for their survival. An interesting picture arises. On the one hand, these enterprises have adjusted a lot, and they have obviously built up a substantial potential for further changes. On the other hand, a number of peculiarities and distortions persist, such as the preferential treatment of befriended state enterprises and the maintenance of substantial social services for the employees. State paternalism remains strong.

But what has happened to the standard of living? *Andrei Illarionov*, *Richard Layard* and *Peter Orszag* have gone through all kinds of relevant statistics. They see a substantial decline in average consumption, while food consumption has fallen little. Inequality as well as regional inequality have risen, as generally perceived. The main problem of poverty is to be found in large families, since children's benefits have lagged behind. But unemployment remains low.

My own paper (*Anders Åslund*) compares the economic transformations in Poland and Russia. At present, they look remarkably different. Was it wrong of the Russians to look so much to Poland? A scrutiny of failures and successes suggests that the Russian reformers have benefited from the Polish lessons, though they have not been able to incorporate all of them, notably the Russian transformation programme was much less comprehensive than in Poland. Some Polish experiences have been poorly understood, such as the implications of elections. Poland offered no precedent on how to treat the ruble zone. In privatization Russia has learnt much from the Polish mistakes.

The last paper by *Vitaly Naishul* is somewhat different in its nature, since it is a programmatic paper, suggesting a highly liberal policy for Russia. Naishul's view is that the Russian state is so weak at present that it can hardly do anything properly. Therefore, it should withdraw to such activities that only the state can carry out properly, primarily law and order. This paper is a telling reflection of a new direction in Russian political and economic thinking.

How should we look upon the Russian economic transformation? Is it a failure or a success? Today, it might appear easy to declare it a failure and state that nothing that has led to 2,500 per cent inflation (in 1992) and an official decline in GNP of almost 40 per cent can be anything but a miserable failure. However, the obvious response is to ask for a realistic alternative. In Ukraine, we see how dangerous it is not to act vigorously for a fundamental economic and political transformation, and in Estonia and Latvia we see apparent successes, despite massive structural changes. After all, much has already been accomplished in Russia. My personal suspicion is that a successful turn in Russia's politics, and thus in its economic policies, will cast a favourable light also upon what has been. But if Russia experiences a political back-lash, the current indeterminate period can look as bad as Weimar Germany.

*Anders Åslund*
*Stockholm and Moscow*

# 1 Prospects for Russian Stabilization in the Summer of 1993

*Stanley Fischer**

The first 18 months of the Russian reform program present a thoroughly mixed picture. On the positive side: privatization is well launched; the retail distribution sector is expanding rapidly; the foreign exchange market is operating and expanding; the West has twice proclaimed its willingness to provide large sums of aid in support of Russian reform and stabilization; the Central Bank and the Government have agreed that credit growth will be reduced, with the aim of reaching an inflation rate of 5 percent by December; and most important, this period has sharpened the understanding in Russia and abroad of the key reforms still needed in the economy, and of what it will take to stabilize it. On the negative side: inflation proceeds apace; price liberalization is only partial, and not advancing; foreign trade remains heavily regulated; aid is being wasted by the heavy subsidization of imports financed through foreign export credits; the budget situation is tenuous, as are lines of authority among different levels of fiscal authority; foreign investment regulations are at best confused; and the list could be extended.

At this point, the economy seems to have settled into a quasi-stable equilibrium, with inflation, industrial production, the real wage, real consumer expenditure, and the real exchange rate all being reasonably steady (Table 1.1). Industrial production has stabilized at about 80 percent of the December 1991 level, and about 65-70 percent of its peak, attained in 1989. Reported consumption has declined to less than half its level at the start of 1991, a greater decline than that of real wages.[1]

The real value of both currency and M2 holdings fell precipitously when prices were liberalized in January 1992. The real stocks of both have increased since then (Table 1.1): despite the continuing high inflation, there is little evidence from the aggregate data of an unstable inflationary dynamic. However, a closer look at the data shows some signs of potential instability. In particular, household real balances have both declined and shifted almost entirely to currency; and almost 50 percent of enterprise real balances are now held in the form of foreign exchange. Extension of dollarization to currency holdings could unleash the destabilizing forces lying in wait in any inflationary situation: the Keynes-Olivera-Tanzi effect, and the flight from money into foreign currencies and into goods.

**Table 1.1** Basic data

| | 1992.2 | 1992.3 | 1992.4 | 1993.1 | Apr '93 |
|---|---|---|---|---|---|
| Inflation (CPI, % per month) | 18 | 11 | 25 | 24 | 17 |
| Indust. production (Dec'91=100) | 94 | 78 | 80 | 79 | 79 |
| Real wage (1990=100) | 56 | 63 | 68 | 58 | |
| Real cons. exp. (1991.1=100) | 36 | 41 | 45 | 41 | 42 |
| Real exch. rate (Apr'91=100) | 34 | 29 | 42 | 31 | 30 |
| Real curr. holdings (Dec'91=100) | 26 | 39 | 40 | 34 | 34 |
| Real M2 holdings (Dec'91=100) | 21 | 29 | 31 | 25 | |

*Source*: *Russian Economic Trends*, Monthly Update, 20 May 1993.

In April 1993 the G-7 announced a new $43 billion aid package for Russia. Its most important innovation is the IMF's Systemic Transformation Facility (STF), which allows the Fund to make loans before the full conditions for a stand-by have been met. The use of the STF could break the deadlock in which the West has in principle been willing to provide aid to Russia provided she undertakes a stabilization program, while Russia appears to have needed the aid to start flowing into the budget in order to stabilize.

More of the elements are in place for a stabilization effort now than at any time in the last 18 months. The Finance Ministry and the Central Bank have already reached agreements on the control of credit growth and on interest rates. These pacts are the core of the gradualist stabilization program, on the basis of which the Russian government is likely to reach agreements with the IMF for the use of first the STF, and then a regular stand-by.

I start this paper by reviewing the program of the Russian government and the analysis that underlies it. I conclude by arguing that within a few months the Russian government will be able to undertake a coordinated exchange-rate based stabilization program which aims to bring the inflation rate down almost immediately to the 3–5 percent per month range, and that it should do so.

## 1 The stabilization program

The stabilization program of the Russian government is based on four pillars: 1) Sharp reductions in credit growth by the Central Bank of Russia (CBR); 2) A reduction in the budget deficit, brought about through lower spending and higher revenues; 3) The use of foreign financing to cover most of the budget deficit and to provide funds to enterprises which previously received subsidized credits from the CBR and government ministries; and 4) Further, though still incomplete, price and trade liberalization.

The diagnosis of the current situation is that massive and excessive credit growth has been the prime cause of inflation. Most of that credit growth has gone to subsidize enterprises (Table 2) and some has gone to support the budget. While much of the gross credit provided to the enterprise sector has been offset by the inflation tax on firms (to be discussed below), the reform strategy assumes that, given the state of the banking system and private sector saving, it will not be possible to finance the enterprise sector without an injection of non-private sector funds. Since such funds cannot come from the CBR if inflation is to be reduced, they will have to come through the budget, ultimately from the external sector. In the credit plan for the remainder of 1993 (Table 3), the CBR will stop making loans to other republics. If any loans are to be made to those republics, they should be made through the budget.

**Table 1.2** Central Bank credit flows, 1992 (% of GDP)

| | | |
|---|---|---|
| Total | | 40 |
| Budget | | 8 |
| Enterprises | | 22 |
| via commercial banks | 16 | |
| via Finance Ministry | 6 | |
| Other republics | | 10 |

In addition to excessive credit growth, the budget deficit has been very large (Table 1.4). This applies less to the domestic budget than to the budget including foreign exchange subsidies, which amounted in 1992 to nearly 13 percent of GDP. This subsidization of imports means that foreign credits have not contributed to the financing of the domestic budget deficit, and also means that domestic industries have been adversely affected by subsidized competitive imports.

**Table 1.3** Planned Central Bank credit flows (% of GDP)

| | | Budget | Enterprises | Other Republics | Total |
|---|---|---|---|---|---|
| 1993 | Q2 | 7 | 8 | 1 | 16 |
| | Q3 | 6 | 5 | 0 | 11 |
| | Q4 | 5 | 2 | 0 | 7 |

The government is proposing to cut the budget deficit, including foreign exchange subsidies, from 20 percent of GDP in 1992 to 10 percent in 1993, and 8 percent in the fourth quarter. To achieve this, it is proposing a 4 percent increase in revenue (relative to 1992), cuts in subsidies to the coal sector, grain producers, and imports, and reductions in interest rate subsidies. The biggest single category of deficit reduction is the proposed 9.5 percent of GDP reduction in unbudgeted import subsidies.

The government's stabilization program recognizes that export quotas and price controls, especially on oil, need to be removed. It recognizes further that energy price increases could help reduce the budgetary gap, and shows an increase in revenues from oil taxation of nearly 4 percent of GDP over the course of 1993. The government proposes removing all export quotas by the end of 1993, except on oil, gas, and some oil products, which are to be lifted by the end of 1994. Presumably the lifting of quotas will be related to the removal of price controls on these products. Domestic prices would then be tied to world prices, with the possibility that export taxes would leave a gap between domestic and foreign prices.

The government's intention is to bring the inflation rate down below 10 percent per month by the end of the year – indeed the target for December is 5 percent. While it aims to continue unifying and expanding the foreign exchange market, it will not commit to a stable exchange rate until the inflation rate has been substantially reduced.

In the remainder of the paper we will review the elements of the stabilization plan in more detail, and then discuss its overall coherence. Among the questions that need to be considered are whether the planned deficit reduction will be adequate for stabilization, what will be the alternate sources of financing for the enterprise sector, the question of whether and at what point the exchange rate might be fixed, and the question of the sequencing of price liberalization relative to other measures. We will also consider the role of western financial assistance.

**Table 1.4** Fiscal data (% of GDP)

| | 1992 (actual) | 1993.1 (prel.) | 1993.4 (plan) |
|---|---|---|---|
| 1 Revenue | | | |
| Total | 30.8 | 40.1 | 34.4 |
| VAT | 11.8 | 12.0 | 9.4 |
| Domestic tax on oil | 0.5 | 1.2 | 4.3 |
| Profit tax | 9.2 | 14.5 | 7.7 |
| Household income tax | 2.5 | 2.9 | 1.7 |
| Export tax | 1.8 | 3.2 | 2.5 |
| Import tariffs | 0.3 | 1.3 | 1.4 |
| 2 Expenditures, cash | | | |
| Total | 40.8 | 49.2 | 40.7 |
| Wage bill | 6.4 | 9.5 | 13.0 |
| Prod.& cons.subsidies | 8.1 | 9.2 | 4.4 |
| Ops.& maintenance | 7.3 | 9.6 | 6.2 |
| Investment | 2.9 | 3.5 | 5.6 |
| Foreign expenditure | 3.1 | 5.0 | 5.5 |
| Defense (incl.wages) | 5.0 | 7.6 | 5.7 |
| Net lending for working capital | 3.5 | -0.2 | -0.1 |
| Other | 4.5 | 5.0 | 0.4 |
| 3 Extrabudgetary funds | 2.6 | 2.5 | 1.4 |
| 4 General government balance | -7.3 | -6.6 | -4.9 |
| 5 Unbudgeted import subsidies | 12.6 | 5.1 | 3.1 |
| 6 Enlarged deficit, cash | -20.0 | -11.7 | -8.0 |
| 7 Financing | | | |
| Foreign | 12.8 | 5.4 | 5.9 |
| Domestic | 7.1 | 6.3 | 2.1 |
| Float | | 3.8 | -0.4 |
| Domestic bank finance | 6.0 | 2.5 | 7.1 |
| CBR | | 3.3 | 6.4 |
| Memo | | | |
| Surplus of local governments | 1.7 | 4.1 | 2.7 |

## 2 Credit growth and credit policy

The proximate causes of inflation are summarized in Figure 1.1, an extension of a chart by Jeffrey Sachs.[2] The rate of inflation in Russia is related to money (M2) growth, lagged three months.[3] While persuasive to the eye, the relationship is not very strong ($R^2 = 0.24$), but that should not be surprising given the limited degrees of freedom afforded by the short data series. The relationship between M2 and inflation is stronger than that between currency growth (lagged two months) and inflation, seen in Figure 1.2 ($R^2 = 0.19$), or between the growth rate of central bank credit and inflation, seen in Table 1.3.[4]

The three-month lag in Figure 1.1 is quite short by the standards of monetarist relations in more stable economies, where lags are generally between 6 and 18 months. The lags shorten in high inflations. The effects here, if they are causal, probably come through the direct impact of increased money growth on the exchange rate, and in part, as argued by Sachs, through the link between credit growth and wages in state-owned enterprises. Neither of these relationships appears clearly in simple regressions using recent Russian data, but the difficulty of detecting the relationship empirically is probably due to the shortness of the data series. There

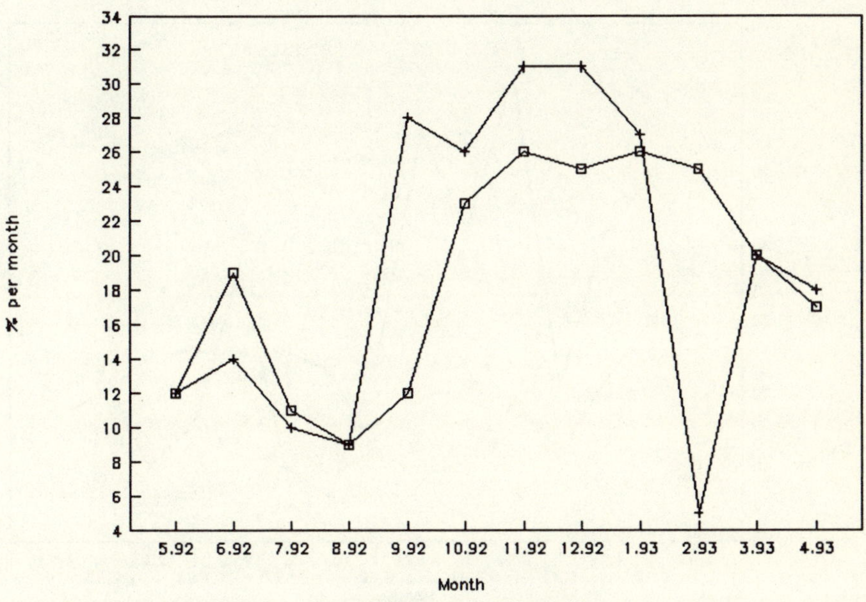


**Figure 1.1** Russia: inflation and money growth (M2 growth lagged 3 months)

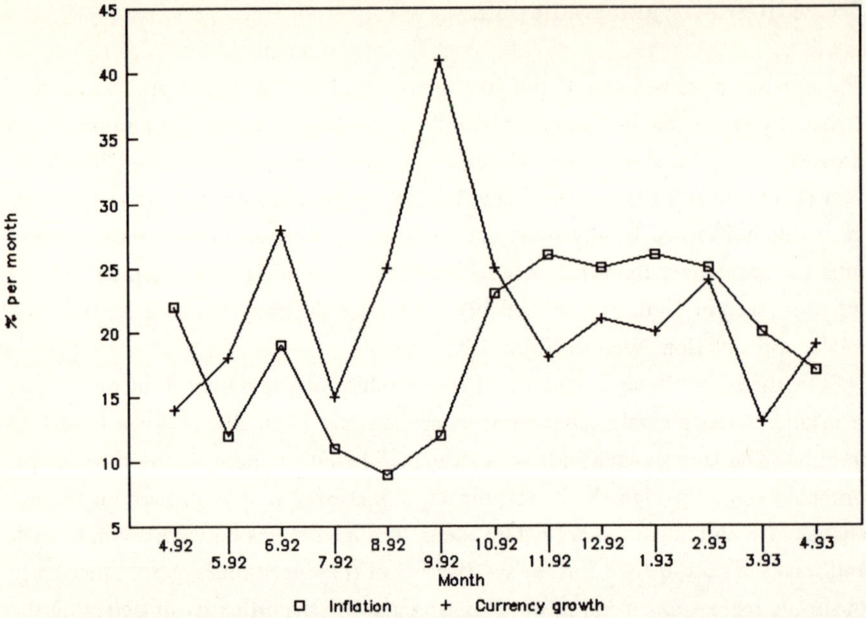


**Figure 1.2** Russia: inflation and currency growth (currency growth lagged 2 months)

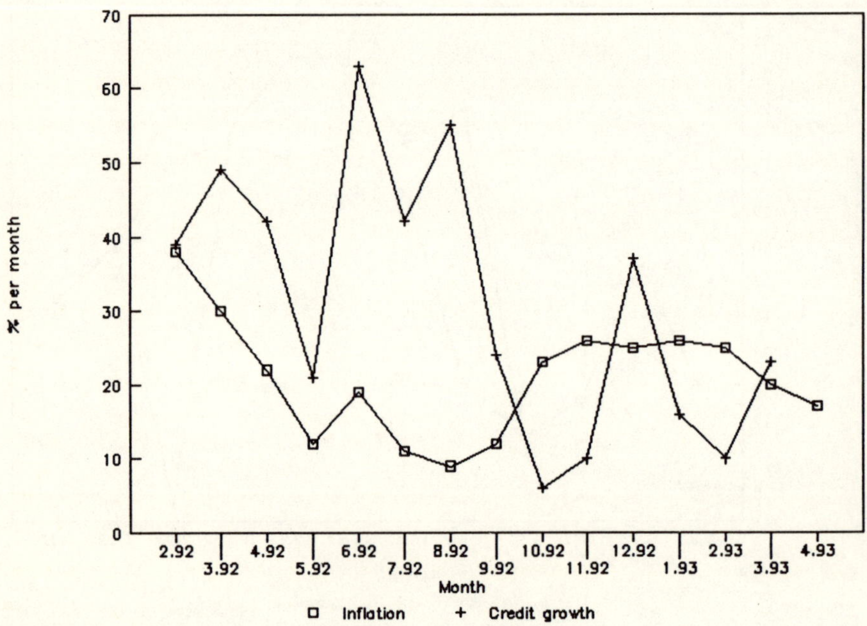


**Figure 1.3** Russia: inflation and credit growth (CBR credit)

is also a direct valuation feedback from changes in the exchange rate to M2 measured in rubles, since foreign currency deposits represent a substantial (and increasing) share of M2. In any case, whatever the precise mechanisms, there can be no doubt that inflation will not be sharply reduced unless money and credit growth are cut back.

Figure 1.1 confirms that in Russia as elsewhere, inflation is a monetary phenomenon. But, as everywhere, money growth is not exogenous, and to stop or slow money growth, the Russian government will have to cut off the flows of central bank credit into the economy – either by dealing with their causes or by finding alternative sources of financing. Table 1.2 presents data on the distribution of Central Bank of Russia (CBR) credit flows in 1992.[5]

The rate of central bank credit creation as a share of GDP was an extraordinary 40 percent in 1992. More than half that amount went to enterprises, some of it through the Finance Ministry. Thus, as the Central Bank points out from time to time, it created credit partly in response to government requests. In addition, the CBR provided credits worth 10 percent of GDP to other republics, to finance imports from Russia. In the first quarter of 1993, the aggregate amount of credit provided by the CBR declined to about 27 percent of GDP, mainly because of a decline in financing for the government.[6]

In May the CBR and the Ministry of Finance signed a pact committing the CBR to reduce the rate of credit creation to 10 percent per month by the end of the year, with a target inflation rate of 5 percent per month. The amount of credit to be provided as a share of GDP is shown in Table 1.3. Central Bank credit to the other republics will be cut to zero by the end of the second quarter, and direct Central Bank credit to enterprises will have been reduced from 26 percent of GDP to 2 percent at the end of this year.

The planned cutoff of Central Bank credit to other republics is consistent with the introduction of independent currencies, which have been or are likely to be introduced in most of the other republics of the former Soviet Union. Several republics, including Kazakhstan, have decided to remain in the ruble area, while others are in the intermediate phase in which both the ruble and coupons circulate domestically. Presumably any aid from Russia to those countries that remain in the ruble area, or to any other republic, will be funnelled through the budget.[7] For those countries with independent currencies, exchange rates will adjust to deal with payments imbalances. Presumably there are procedures for dealing with any republic in the ruble area that is running a deficit with Russia.

At the same time as the quantity of credit provided is reduced, it will also be necessary to begin raising its real cost. The CBR plans increasingly to use market mechanisms, for instance a credit auction, to change the quantity of credit, and thus to set its price. The CBR will likely also have to operate a discount window, but the rate at that window can be set by reference to the rate in the credit auction, for instance as a small fixed markup over the market rate.[8]

Wherever nominal interest rates are set by the government, the aim should be to raise them to a positive real level gradually. At the same time, the real interest rate on deposits needs to be raised to the point where households will want to hold these assets, and thereby increase the flow of financial intermediation. The CBR will have to decide whether deposit rates will be regulated or allowed to be set by competition; if the latter, it is crucial to exercise prudential regulation of the banks, to ensure that implicit or explicit deposit insurance does not lead to excessive risk-taking by the commercial banks.

The Russian government is apparently intending to continue subsidizing some credit, using the Commission on Credit Policy to make decisions on where the subsidies are to be provided, and including the subsidies in the budget. The government states that it will reduce these subsidies to less than one percent of GDP this year, and that it will not make allocations for working capital. This would certainly represent a major improvement relative to 1992, when the budget is estimated to have provided interest subsidies to firms of about 2.5 percent of GDP.

Three key questions emerge from the discussion of credit policy. First, are the amounts of credit growth targeted for the end of 1993 consistent with low inflation? Second, what will be the impact on firms of the sharp cutoff of CBR credit, and what are the alternative sources of credit? And finally, will the agreed credit targets be achieved? To answer these questions, we need to turn to fiscal policy and the role of the inflation tax in Russia.

## 3 Fiscal policy

Budgets for 1992, preliminary data for the first quarter of 1993, and the planned budget for the last quarter of this year are presented in Table 1.4. Two facts stand out. The first is the correspondence in 1992 and the first quarter of 1993 between the size of net import subsidies and foreign financing. To a first approximation, foreign financing has not so far been used to finance the domestic budget deficit.

The second is the absence so far of non-bank financing, for example through the sale of Treasury bills.

In relying on Central Bank financing to cover the deficit, the Russian government has been using seigniorage to finance its expenditures (broadly defined), and imposing the inflation tax as the counterpart of the seigniorage. In 1992, the monetary base increased by 5.5 trillion rubles, in a year in which nominal GDP was 17 trillion rubles. This implies total seigniorage revenues of approximately 30 percent of GDP.[9] Of course, this far exceeds central bank financing of the deficit, for the obvious reason that much of the monetary expansion financed other republics and especially enterprises.

The inflation tax is customarily calculated as the product of the monetary base and the inflation rate.[10] By the end of 1992, the monetary base was approximately 16 percent of GDP.[11] Assuming the inflation rate was 22 percent per month, the annualized continuously compounded rate would be approximately 240 percent per annum. This implies an inflation tax of as much as 38 percent of GDP. If we assume that the household portion of this tax is the loss in real value of currency holdings, the inflation tax on households amounts to approximately 12 percent of GDP. In fact, the household inflation tax is somewhat higher, because interest rates on ruble accounts are well below the inflation rate, and households continue to hold some bank accounts.

The remainder of the inflation tax is levied on enterprises, which are also in aggregate the major beneficiaries of CBR credit creation. According to the present calculations, enterprises would have paid an inflation tax of around 25 percent of GDP, and received CBR credits of approximately the same amount in 1992. This suggests that on balance and in aggregate, credit creation essentially compensated enterprises for the inflation tax they paid, a conclusion reached earlier by Jeffrey Sachs (*op.cit*). However, the calculations are not precise, and a related calculation by Richard Layard suggests that the enterprise sector gained from inflation, perhaps by as much as 10 percent of GDP.

The aggregate outcome is of some interest, because if a net transfer of 10 percent of GDP were taken away from firms, it would create difficulties and political pressures that could not be ignored. But the right perspective is somewhat different. It starts by recognizing that within the enterprise sector there were certainly both gainers and losers from the credit creation-inflation nexus, and that the ending of this process will no doubt cause major difficulties to the firms that were benefiting from the inflationary process. Obviously, the solution is not to compensate all those who will lose when credit growth is brought under control, but to put in place mechanisms and systems that will enable those firms that should get credit to receive it. We will return to this issue in discussing the proposed enterprise funds.

What fiscal changes would need to be made for inflation to decline to the 3-5 percent per month range that could be regarded as success on the inflation front? Assuming a monetary base of 10 percent of GDP, no real growth of output, and an annual inflation rate of 40 percent, seigniorage would amount to 3.4 percent of GDP. To collect double that amount, 7 percent of GDP, the annual inflation rate would have to be at least 100 percent – and this is a highly optimistic estimate, since it assumes the demand for real monetary base would not be shifting in response to ongoing inflation.

Even the estimate of 3.4 percent of GDP as being consistent with 40 percent inflation is optimistic in the light of dollarization and other ruble-economizing changes that are bound to continue if inflation persists. It is rare for governments in slow-growth economies to collect more than 3 percent of GDP in seigniorage. Most likely, the Russian government should be aiming for money financing and Central Bank credit creation of no more than 2.5 percent of GDP.

However, the existence of large excess reserves in the banking system means that inflation could continue for some time even after credit growth is slowed. Some estimates suggest the price level could more than double purely on the basis of a runoff of excess reserves, but it is possible that these reserves are being voluntarily held, and that the inflationary threat they pose is exaggerated.[12]

The seigniorage analysis implies that any budget deficit in excess of 2.5 percent of GDP would have to be financed by non-monetary means, the sale of either domestic assets, or foreign exchange. Domestic assets could be privatization proceeds, which however have been very small, and are likely to continue to be small. In addition, the government could sell Treasury bills or bonds. While the government plans to introduce Treasury bills, and shows financing of as much as 0.7 percent of GDP from this source in the more detailed table that underlies Table 1.4, the market for government paper will be very weak until stabilization is attained, and the credibility of government commitments increases. But if stabilization occurs, and if the government pays a positive real interest rate, then there is no reason that the market for government securities should not develop rapidly. Indeed, it is quite likely that there would in the early stages be a capital inflow if the government were to stabilize using an exchange rate anchor: typically in exchange-rate based stabilizations in which credit has been tightened sharply, the domestic real interest rate rises, and with the exchange rate fixed, domestic assets pay high yields relative to similar foreign assets.

The short-term key, though, is foreign financing of the budget deficit. Over the past 18 months, the emphasis on the role of foreign aid has changed. Foreign financing is increasingly seen as being needed to finance the domestic budget deficit in a non-inflationary way, rather than to finance an import surplus. But of course these two elements cannot be separated. If the capital account of the private sector were balanced throughout, any increase in foreign financing would have to be associated with an increased current account deficit. Alternatively, the increased financing of the current account could be associated with an increase in the private sector capital outflow – but that would hardly be the aim of the government borrowing.

In the case of Russia, though, there is a very well-defined sense in which foreign funding can be used to finance the budget deficit *without increasing the current account deficit*. Specifically, last year and in the first quarter of 1993, export credits were used essentially to subsidize imports: in 1992 unbudgeted import subsidies amounted to 12.6 percent of GDP, almost exactly equal to the 12.8 percent of GDP foreign financing of the budget deficit; in the first quarter of 1992 the corresponding numbers are 5.1 percent of GDP and 5.4 percent respectively. Thus the foreign financing barely contributed to financing of the domestic budget deficit.

Could foreign export credits have been used better? Some of these credits were provided to Russian importers at an exchange rate that made the import price lower even than the domestic price. That was clearly a waste. In the case of grains, the foreign exchange was provided at an exchange rate that made the imported price the same as the domestic price. In this case it is possible that the Russian government would not have been able to sell the foreign exchange tied to the import of these goods at a higher price.[13]

Even in the latter case, though, it is clear that the foreign exchange that Russia was borrowing was in an important sense being wasted; had the domestic prices of these goods been closer to the world level, then the foreign exchange could have been sold at a higher price. It may be that at a higher price there would not have been domestic demand for the imports. If that were the case, then the question is why it made sense for Russia to borrow in order to provide subsidized imports.[14]

In any case, the Russian government is planning to make major cuts in import subsidies. The plan is for import subsidies to decline to 3.1 percent of GDP in the fourth quarter, compared with 12.6 percent last year. This change will by itself significantly reduce the overall budget deficit.

The G-7 aid package promised in April 1993 is summarized in Table 1.5. The planned budget shows foreign financing of the deficit of 5.9 percent of GDP, meaning that foreign finance would make a net contribution of 2.8 percent of GDP to the budget, covering more than half of the general government balance of 4.9 percent.[15] That leaves a deficit of only 2.1 percent of GDP to be covered by domestic financing. We have already calculated that seigniorage can safely cover a deficit of as much as 2.5 percent of GDP. This suggests that the planned budget in Table 1.4 is indeed consistent with a low inflation equilibrium.[16]

**Table 1.5** G-7 aid package ($ bn)

| | | |
|---|---|---|
| Initial stabilization support | | 4.1 |
| of which: | | |
| IMF Systemic Transformation Facility | 3.0 | |
| IBRD import rehabilitation loan | 1.1 | |
| Full stabilization program | | 10.1 |
| of which: | | |
| IMF stand-by | 4.1 | |
| Stabilization fund | 6.0 | |
| Structural reform and essential imports | | 14.2 |
| of which: | | |
| IBRD loan commitments | 3.4 | |
| Cofinancing of World Bank oil sector loan | 0.5 | |
| EBRD enterprise fund | 0.3 | |
| Export credit/guarantees | 10.0 | |
| Public debt rescheduling | | 15.0 |
| Total | | 43.4 |

*Source*: *Transition*, World Bank, April 1993, p.1

What could go wrong? First, the budget deficit at 8 percent of GDP is large. Second, the budget is premised on a number of domestic policy actions that have so far been difficult to take: oil prices are to rise, import subsidies are to be cut, production and consumption subsidies are to be cut by 4 percent of GDP, net lending for working capital is to be cut. All these extremely difficult decisions have to be in place by the end of the third quarter, if the planned budget is to be implemented. Third, it remains to be seen whether the ambitious credit targets of Table 1.3 will be implemented. In particular, these targets assume an almost complete cutoff of central bank financing for both other republics and enterprises. Fourth, it is not certain that the foreign financing will be agreed and disbursed on the schedule shown in Table 1.6.

**Table 1.6** Potential flows of foreign support, 1993 ($ bn)

| | Q2 | Q3 | Q4 |
|---|---|---|---|
| IMF STF | 1.5 | 1.5 | |
| IBRD imp. rehab. loan | 0.6 | 0.5 | |
| IMF standby | | | 1.5 |
| IBRD project loans | | 0.6 | 0.6 |
| EBRD | | 0.1 | 0.1 |
| Import credits/grants | 0.5 | 4.3 | 1.9 |
| Total | 2.6 | 7.0 | 4.1 |
| As % of GDP | 10.4 | 21.0 | 10.1 |

The risks could be reduced if the planned budget deficit were cut, both by reducing import subsidies, and by moving energy prices more rapidly towards world levels. These policy measures should be taken not only to reduce the budget deficit, and to provide the right price incentives, but also because delaying these adjustments reduces the likelihood that stabilization will be successful. By leaving some of these adjustments to be made later, the government ensures that major inflationary shocks will occur after the stabilization program goes into effect. It is far better to get the shocks over with before the stabilization than to leave them waiting to happen, thereby both threatening whatever stabilization has been achieved, and providing one more excuse for not making the necessary price changes.

Implementation of the planned budget will require greater political strength than the Russian government has yet been able to demonstrate – not only in relations between the Finance Ministry and the rest of the central government, but also in relations between the government and enterprises, and between the central government and the regional governments. The President's decisive victory in the April referendum may have brought him the necessary political strength.

## 4 Enterprise financing

The reduction of CBR credit creation, and cutbacks in interest subsidies from the Government, will reduce gross flows to the enterprise sector by nearly 30 percent of GDP. The net reduction will be much smaller, perhaps as much as 10-12 percent of GDP, perhaps as little as 5 percent.

Whatever the extent of the reduction, the question remains what financing will be available for investment and restructuring by and of Russian enterprises. The domestic banking system is certainly capable of providing some financing, and will be more capable of doing so if the inflation rate comes down, and households begin to place saving in the financial system. But it is unlikely that the banking system will be in a position to provide long-term financing on any significant scale. Nor is there much to be hoped for yet from any stock exchange, although the privatization process may help develop securities trading.

The Government of Russia, supported by the United States, is seeking to establish a series of enterprise funds, financed from abroad, that will provide long-term financing for restructuring companies. There are controversies over whether such funding should be made available only to privatized companies, or also to companies in the state sector, and also controversies over who should administer these funds.

Those are not questions we need go into in this paper. But we do need to note that both the economic and the political success of the stabilization program depend on the creation of such funds, or their equivalent. Without funding, companies that could and should survive in the market economy might not do so. Politically, after the referendum and perhaps with a new constitution, Russia may be able to put up with more plant closings and restructurings. But the system will not be able to resist populist pressures to keep failing companies alive if it is not possible to point to a rational process that enables firms that should survive to do so.

## 5 Stabilization: gradualism and the big bang

The Russian government has set out a gradualist stabilization program that aims to reduce credit growth, liberalize prices, and reduce trade restrictions over the next 9–12 months. The planned budget for the last quarter of 1993, and presumably the budget for 1994, as well as the plans for credit creation, are consistent with

3-5 percent per month inflation. The measures needed to attain these budget and credit goals are also understood.

Thus, the elements of a coherent stabilization program have been laid out here. The key question that remains is whether the Russian government should pursue the gradualist approach that it has laid out, or should rather at an appropriate time attempt to move the economy rapidly to low inflation.

In the current Russian context, where it is very unclear what changes can actually be made, the gradualist approach has much to commend it. Over the next six months, the government should be moving rapidly to liberalize prices, raise energy prices, lift export restrictions, and stop subsidizing imports, at the same time as it fast reduces CBR credit creation. If it is to succeed in cutting credit growth, it will have to have set up enterprise funds.

A gradualist program that makes all these changes will certainly help move the economy towards a sustainable real equilibrium. However, such a program is unlikely to move the inflation rate down decisively. There is too much momentum in the economy, and too many places at which the program can go off the rails, to leave Russian stabilization to gradualism.

Gradualist programs have rarely been successful in finally stabilizing inflation. But most of the changes set out by the Government of Russia have to be undertaken. Accordingly, the program should start with the gradualist approach set out above. That phase should be over by the end of September 1993. Provided most of the structural measures specified above have been made, the government could then move to the second stage of the stabilization program, in which it fixes the exchange rate and brings inflation down to the range of 3–5 percent per month. To support the fixing of the exchange rate, it would draw on the stabilization fund, that has been waiting to be activated for well over a year.

This could all be done before the end of 1993, indeed even early in the fourth quarter. If the major price and trade adjustments are made before the exchange rate is fixed, such a program would have an excellent chance of succeeding, that is, of bringing inflation down to 40–60 percent per annum. Given the massive undervaluation of the ruble, the nominal exchange rate could easily be held at its initial level for at least a year, giving the exchange rate anchor time to slow the inflationary process, and thereby enable the restructuring of the economy to take place in an environment of relative price and macroeconomic stability.

Aside perhaps from the Bolivian case, there has been no successful stabilization in the last decade that did not stabilize by using an exchange rate anchor. All the recent successful stabilization and economic reform programs have been headed by and associated with a single official, usually the Finance Minister, working with a small team of trusted (usually young) advisers, who monitor the operation of the program in the various ministries. Usually the Central Bank supports the program vigorously, and successful programs have the strong and active support of the President or Prime Minister.

One of the major benefits of undertaking a stabilization program of this type, rather than a gradualist program, is that it concentrates the minds of policy makers, and thereby improves decision making. With a gradualist program, no particular policy measure is crucial, and there is always time to wait for necessary actions to be taken – with the result that the key decisions continue to be delayed, and the economy continues operating at a lower level than necessary for longer than necessary. Once it is planned to undertake a coherent, exchange-rate based, stabilization program, a sense of urgency pervades the decision-making process and helps get decisions made.

The data reviewed in this paper show that Russia is now within hailing distance of being able to undertake such a program within a few months. The economic resources to support such a process are present, and the political support is increasingly evident. It is widely recognized that the inflation should be ended. The opportunity is here, but there is no guarantee that circumstances will keep the opportunity open. It is time to prepare for action, by early autumn at the latest.

## Notes

* I am grateful to Richard Layard, Jeffrey Sachs and Paulo Vieira da Cunha for helpful conversations, and to the National Science Foundation for research support.

1. Two comments: first, the inflation tax on households helps account for the greater decline in consumption than real wages; and second, it is quite likely that the official data underestimate purchases of consumption goods. This latter view is taken by Andrei Illarionov, Richard Layard and Peter Orszag in chapter 9 of this volume.
2. Jeffrey Sachs, "Achieving Monetary Stabilization in Russia in 1993", mimeo, March 1993.
3. M2 consists of currency in circulation plus all deposits of households and firms in commercial banks, plus household deposits in Sberbank.
4. Since no particular lag is evident, we show the contemporaneous relationship.
5. These data were made available by Jeffrey Sachs. An alternate series by Richard Layard puts budget financing at 4 percent of GDP and enterprise financing at 26 percent.
6. This decline may be seasonal, since the government ran a surplus in the first quarter of 1992 as well as 1993.

7. Recently, ruble banknotes have been sent to other countries without charge. Such shipments provide credit, and should be counted against the agreed credit targets.
8. The government and the CBR have agreed that the CBR finance rate will be no more than 7 percent *below* the interbank rate. This still represents a subsidized rate for credit. The CBR should increasingly charge a penal rate for borrowing, above the interbank rate, to tighten its control over the monetary base and the quantity of money.
9. The calculation is approximate because it takes no account of the timing of seigniorage flows during the year. A better measure would calculate the integral of the real value of seigniorage during the year, and divide it by real GDP.
10. In this case, the correct magnitude is the integral of the product of the monetary base and the inflation rate at each instant over the course of the year.
11. The calculation assumes real GDP was constant during the first quarter of 1993, and then works back from estimated nominal GDP for that quarter (12.6 trillion, at a quarterly rate) to an estimate of nominal GDP at the end of 1992, using monthly inflation rates and assuming inflation was uniform during each month.
12. In 1937, the Fed raised reserve requirements to get rid of excess reserves in the banking system. Because the reserves were desired and not really excess, this led to a credit crunch that contributed to the 1937 recession.
13. I am indebted to Richard Layard for discussion of this point.
14. Alternatively, if world agricultural markets were reasonably open, Russia could in principle have increased net exports at the same time as it borrowed abroad to finance imports. However, international agricultural markets are not open and the suppliers of agricultural export credits would be unlikely to welcome their use to increase Russian exports.
15. The 5.9 percent of GDP in foreign financing shown in Table 1.4 is much smaller than the 10 percent shown in Table 1.6. The conservatism shown in Table 1.4 is probably appropriate, since there is very likely to be serious slippage in the timing of several of the large loans shown in Table 1.6.
16. The 6.4 percent of financing shown as coming from the CBR in Table 1.4 includes most of the foreign financing, so it does *not* correspond to an increase in the money base by 6.4 percent of GDP.

# 2 1993: The First Experiences of the Russian Financial and Monetary Stabilization Policy

*Boris G. Fedorov and Andrei I. Kazmin*

Price liberalization, the privatization of state-owned enterprises and the termination of administrative restrictions on retail and wholesale trade were the crucial achievements of economic policy in 1992. These factors gave a powerful impulse to the whole reform process in Russia, but they were not enough to guarantee its irreversibility. Without financial stabilization, any further progress in economic transformation became questionable.

By the end of 1992 and in the first quarter of 1993 the situation appeared to be critical. The inflation rate reached the threatening level of 30 percent per month, and the budget deficit (including non-budgetary funds) comprised nearly 20 percent of the GDP. At the same time the foreign indebtedness increased up to $80 bn and state gold and hard currency reserves were exhausted.

Under these circumstances the renewed governmental program of economic reforms declared financial stabilization as the chief priority for 1993. The specified targets of the program included a quarterly reduction of centralized credits by 10 percent, drastic budget cuts in order to minimise the yearly deficit to 5 percent of the GDP and a reduction of the inflation rate down to one-digit levels on a monthly basis by the end of the year.

The first attempts to implement this ambitious program were strongly opposed by the agro-industrial lobby within the government and the Supreme Soviet and by the conservative leadership of the Central Bank of Russia (CBR). The abnormal and useless confrontation between the two main bodies responsible for monetary and credit policy, namely the Ministry of Finance and the CBR, has in fact blocked all attempts to clean up the mess in the credit and financial sector during the first half of the year.

Under substantial pressure from the IMF, the CBR was forced to co-operate with the Ministry of Finance in setting quarterly limits for the expansion of centralized credits in order to reduce the inflation rate down to a one-digit level on a monthly basis by the end of 1993. Reviewing the achieved results, one has to assume that the bilateral Commitment signed by the Government and the CBR on 22 May, 1993 has played a very important role in the overall tightening of budget constraints and reaffirming of control over the financial situation.

According to this Commitment the CBR was obliged to switch from the disbursement of centralized credits to market forms of re-financing of commercial banks. The basic interest rate of the CBR was consistently increased up to 210 percent per annum, which actually means a positive interest rate, considering that interest payments are collected monthly on a pre-payment basis.[1] Beginning with the second quarter the overall increase in the CBR credits to both the government and commercial banks was limited every quarter by specified targets fixed by the Government Commission on Credit Policy. Since then, the requests of particular enterprises and branches for direct credits have been considered by the Commission and not by the CBR alone as before.

**Table 2.1** Quarterly increase in centralized credits of the CBR, 1993 (bn rubles)

| | | Q I | Q II | Q III | Q IV |
|---|---|---|---|---|---|
| Total increase (net) | | | | | |
| (planned): | | 3500 | 2890 | 4040 | 3614 |
| including: | Government | 1100 | 1373 | 2347 | 2569 |
| | economy | 1100 | 1277 | 1693 | 1045 |
| | CIS countries | 1300 | 240 | — | — |
| Total increase (net) | | | | | |
| (factual and estimated[a]) | | 3500 | 3245 | 5407[a] | 6000[b] |
| including: | Government | 1300 | 1365 | 2765[a] | 4000[b] |
| | economy | 1117 | 1695 | 2642[a] | 2000[b] |
| | CIS | 1352 | 806 | — | — |
| interstate-budget credits, | | | | | |
| including rescheduled "technical | | | | | |
| credits", clearing and cash deliveries | | | | 1016 | 230[c] |

*Notes*: [a] preliminary data, [b] corrected limits set by the Credit Commission, [c] estimate

In line with the adopted Commitment Russia has received the first $ 1.5 bn of the Systemic Transformation Facility (STF) credit from the IMF. The disbursement of the second tranche will depend on the fulfilment of the program of financial stabilization. Table 2.1 shows a preliminary evaluation of the fulfilment of the program as concerns the quarterly increase of centralized credits.

Even a brief analysis of the table shows quite definitely that the absolute targets of the bilateral Commitment were not achieved and the radical scenario of the development of the economic situation in 1993 was not accomplished.

The powerful expansion of net CBR credits to both the Government and commercial banks in the third quarter was too high above the respective ceilings, as are the recently corrected targets for the fourth quarter, which even so will be very hard to reach.

On the basis of these disappointing facts it would be possible to conclude that the declared policy of financial stabilization has failed. No wonder that the special mission of the IMF which visited Moscow in September 1993 stated that the main targets of the Commitment had not been attained and it postponed the decision on the second tranche of the STF credit until a better future.

However, taking into account the political and economic realities of 1993 it would not be correct just to confirm the failure of the financial stabilization due to the reasons mentioned. Learning from our own experience it is now evident that the one-digit inflation rate per month by the end of the year was too optimistic a forecast.

While elaborating the anti-inflation program for 1993 two principal factors were not properly taken into account, which resulted in serious mistakes in the setting of credit ceilings, especially for the third and fourth quarters. First of all, the impact of the traditional seasonality of the Russian economy, caused by the existing system of a centralized supply of fuel, food and goods to the Northern Territories (which comprise 56 out of the 88 subjects of the Russian Federation) and the state monopoly over the procurement of the grain harvest, was strongly underestimated. Secondly, the degree of miscalculation was multiplied due to the spontaneous and substantial increase of state-controlled grain, oil and electricity prices, as well the liberalization of coal prices, and the rise in tariffs for transport and municipal services.

The state remains the biggest consumer of the goods mentioned. Therefore until all administered prices of key goods and services have been liberalized and state-owned property has been decisively shifted to the private sector, peaks of new inflation waves will follow every step toward complete price liberalization. Thus, in the third quarter alone, the amount of centralized credits granted by the Government's Credit Commission for the supply of goods to the Northern Territories exceeded the set limits three-fold and the loans given to the agricultural sector were 30 percent bigger than the planned targets.

Despite sustained attempts to withstand the pressure of the respective lobbies, certain adjustments were made, on the one hand, for socio-political reasons. For example, the price of credit cuts to the Northern Territories would be a massive migration of inhabitants. And on the other hand, there were internal tensions within the Government, accompanied by the provocative policy of the former Supreme Soviet, which welcomed direct illegal appeals from certain members of the cabinet for additional financial injections, despite already existing limits fixed by the Government. The mentioned factors have contributed greatly to the drastic rise in the inflation rate up to 29 percent in August, followed by extraordinary budget and credit cuts in order to reduce inflation to an "acceptable" level of 20 percent.

Beside the failure to reduce the inflation rate and the exceeding of the credit ceilings, which were used as the main argument by the IMF to postpone the second tranche of the STF, several other elements of the Commitment were not implemented in time. Among the most important measures not implemented was that not all directed CBR credits have been channelled through the Credit Commission, in particular, the so-called "credits for emergent regional needs". These loans were disbursed solely by the CBR in rather modest amounts – about 300 bn rubles a quarter (10 percent of disbursed centralized credits), because it is technically impossible to channel them through the Credit Commission on a daily basis. At the adoption of credit targets for the fourth quarter a provisional arrangement was found: the total amount of these credits was included into the overall quarterly limit of the Credit Commission.

The radical aim of phasing out the CBR credits to particular sectors, regions or enterprises was not reached, mainly because of the general weakness of the Russian commercial banks, which lack the capital needed for executing the role of regular creditors of big enterprises and regions. Apart from the problem with their undercapitalization, in some cases banks refuse to channel CBR credits to the determined borrowers, since the huge amounts of transferred money can create problems for their liquidity ratios. Secondly, the banks prefer short and extra-short-term credits, which generate much more profit than the extension of CBR credits to enterprises with lengthy production cycles.

The repayment of the centralized credits is a separate problem, especially for credits extended to agriculture and the Northern Territories. To stimulate debtors to repay on time, the Credit Commission has recently adopted a decision which forbids granting any new credit to those borrowers who have delayed the repayment of previously obtained credits. From now on, to secure the repayment, a minimum of 5 percent of state bonds or T-bills are required in collateral for CBR credits. However, the problem of finding an optimal scheme for financing agriculture and the Northern Territories will not be solved in this way. If an acceptable solution is not found in the nearest future, the next year may also be lost in vain.

The transformation of the Central Bank of Russia into a real central bank remains on the top of the reform agenda. There is no visible progress in the initiation of a flexible interest rate policy. Nor has a normal system of refinancing of the commercial banks been established.

The lack of central bank supervision over the commercial banks is also one of the most burning problems, especially after the CBR's former local and rural branch offices have been transformed into settlement and cash centres, which appears to have been a serious mistake. After this reorganization only the higher branches of the CBR (at oblast, national republic and city level) were authorized to perform banking supervision. As a result, one clerk of the CBR nowadays supervises up to 45–50 commercial banks. This over-concentration of supervisory functions should be abolished, by making the low-level affiliations of the CBR responsible for banking supervision.

Apart from the pure banking problems, one of Russia's most urgent tasks is to build a new system of payments and settlements, while phasing out the accumulated inter-enterprise arrears. Although the real value of inter-enterprise arrears has decreased in comparison to 1992, the situation is far from acceptable.

Therefore, the recently signed Presidential Decree which outlines a general scheme for the elimination of the accumulated inter-enterprise arrears, and the enforced transformation of these into bills of exchange, is of utmost importance. "Financial bills of exchange" (FBOE) will be issued and used as legal liabilities of the debtors for the accumulated indebtedness with a fixed maturity. The issued FBOEs could be used by the holders for mutual clearing for sale on specially organised auctions of bills or for discounting with an appropriate commercial bank. FBOEs are forbidden for rediscount or lombard transactions with the CBR in order to prevent the uncontrolled increase of money in circulation. When maturing, the

FBOEs have to be repaid by the debtor. Otherwise the latter has to be declared insolvent, and a bankruptcy procedure should be applied.

After the old debts have been phased out in the way described, new commercial bills of exchange can be put into circulation. That will settle the problem of the legal inter-enterprise commercial credit and will help a lot in increasing the working capital of enterprises, accelerating payments and developing a civilized system of refinancing of enterprises and commercial banks. To process the elimination of old bad debts and the implementation of the bankruptcy procedures, a special board – the Federal Bankruptcy Agency – has recently been established.

Besides these domestic problems, the recently constructed "ruble zone of a new type" constitutes a powerful factor which can totally change all the forecasts for financial stabilization. Three months after the extraordinary exchange of the "old" ruble notes for new ones, executed by the CBR at the end of July, and the actual separation of the Russian money and credit system from other CIS countries, the situation is far from clear.

The multilateral "Agreement on the Ruble Zone of a New Type" has been signed by Russia, Armenia, Belarus, Kazakhstan, Tajikistan and Uzbekistan. It contains several basic principles. First, a transitional period is considered necessary for the unification of the legislation of the respective republics in the financial, credit, currency and customs areas. Second, the member countries are offered the possibility to issue their own provisional banknotes or to use the "old" rubles as a legal tender on their territories. Third, the currencies of the member countries are supposed to be mutually convertible and they undertake the mutual obligation to sustain the exchange rates on a stable level. Fourth, bilateral Commissions have been formed to coordinate and monitor the progress towards a unified monetary and financial system and the unified currency – the Russian ruble.

However, reasonable principles of a gradual transition to a unified currency were thrown away already in the bilateral agreements of Russia with the respective countries. The CBR has not counted on a lengthy period of circulation of the "old" rubles beyond the Russian borders. Neither has it been concerned with the problem of what kind of banknotes will have to substitute the "old" rubles in circulation in the former Soviet republics after the accumulated stocks of the "old" rubles have been totally drained. Under these conditions the cash crisis has become a real threat to the republics which also suffer from and fear the uncontrolled inundation of "old" rubles from other states of the former Soviet Union (FSU). The claims for immediate deliveries of Russian rubles have intensified sharply, and final targets of the transition period – the achievement of total parity of exchange rates between Russian and non-Russian rubles and the exchange of "old" rubles for Russian ones – have become ultimate political demands.

A lot of arguments speak in favour of a unified currency for Russia and the neighbouring countries. The 3,000 bn ruble debt of the CIS consumers to the Russian exporters, which otherwise will never be paid, is only one example of the pure economic interests on both sides. But many politicians have a strong desire to accelerate the process of economic re-unification, since the idea of a re-integration of the former Soviet Union is still very popular and the coming elections in Russia provide a good opportunity for "unionist" actions without considering the economic consequences of sudden but broadly welcomed political decisions.

If the worst comes and the respective republics receive the Russian rubles in cash, without fulfilling all the necessary preconditions, the idea of a new ruble zone will collapse and the situation prior to July 1993, with unified cash and separate account money, would be reproduced. That will not solve any of the problems of the development of mutual economic co-operation between the CIS countries. After a short relaxation, the inflation rate in Russia will skyrocket, the ruble exchange rate will crash, and intra-CIS trade will decrease. In the end, Russia will once again be forced to exchange cash, but this time without plans for a common currency. The present tactical victory of the other republics will inevitably turn into a total loss and a very costly divorce with Russia in the nearest future.

Critically appraising the year which is drawing to an end, we should not only concentrate on failures, mistakes and unsolved problems. This year convinced the majority of academics and practitioners that economic policy consists up to 75 percent of financial and monetary policy. Households began to feel the importance of the national currency – the ruble, as its purchasing power has visibly improved.

In most regards the implemented financial policy was much more consistent and tight than before; no general netting out of inter-enterprise arrears has been carried out; no inflationary injections into the working capital of state-owned enterprises have been allowed; and all technical credits and uncontrolled cash deliveries to the other CIS countries have been terminated.

The CBR refinance rate, which remained stable from May 1992 until March 1993, has doubled during the last five months. The deposit interest rates with the Savings Bank have also been raised drastically. At the same time, the mechanism of the repatriation of hard currency earnings from exports has also been totally renewed, which helped to stabilize and sustain the exchange rate of the ruble and break inflationary expectations.

These monetary measures were accompanied by a continued liberalization of prices of coal, gas, grain and bread. Nearly all import subsidies were abolished which meant the real implementation of a uniform exchange rate.

The credit constraints were much tighter this year because of the activities of the Government's Credit Commission, which took control over the credit expansion of the Central Bank and managed to reduce the growth of the extended credits in the critical third quarter of the year to one-third of the level of last year.

The severe cuts of budget expenditures render it possible to limit the budget deficit to the promised ceiling of 10 percent of the GNP. Moreover, this year the financing of the budget deficit through issues of securities (T-bills, gold certificates) has begun.

Significant progress in Russia's negotiations with the Paris and London Club and with the G-7 led to debt rescheduling, that helped Russia to obtain credits from the IMF and the World Bank.

The main result, however, is that the situation and economic policy have become more predictable and manageable, though the coming struggle for a tighter budget and stricter credit constraints will be a hard test. The task for the rest of the year is to hold the budget deficit down, continuing to reduce centralized credits in order to reduce the inflation rate down to 15 percent a month by the end of the year (and to one-digit rates in the next year) and to slow down the decrease of the exchange rate of the ruble so that it falls at a rate of half the inflation. A successful finish of the year will help to maintain the first positive results of the financial stabilization in the nearest future – the main argument for the peaceful development of market economy and political democracy in Russia.

## Notes

1. In fact, this means an interest rate of 17.5 percent per month, that is, 593 percent per annum. -Ed.

# 3 Prospects for Monetary Stabilization in Russia

*Jeffrey D. Sachs**

After 18 months of radical economic reforms, Russia continues to suffer from high inflation. Contrary to the intentions of the Russian Government at the start of 1992, and the experience of several Eastern European countries in recent years, Russia's price liberalization was followed by a sustained period of rapid inflation. One year after price liberalization, at the start of 1993, Russia appeared to be headed for hyperinflation, with monthly inflation rates at 30 percent and rising. A tightening of monetary and fiscal policies in the first half of 1993, under the vigorous leadership of Deputy Prime Minister Boris Fedorov, pulled Russia back from the brink of hyperinflation, but the policies have not yet been sufficient to establish price stability.

In May 1993, the Government and Central Bank of Russia (CBR) reached agreement on a goal of cutting the monthly rate of inflation from around 20 percent per month to around 5 percent per month inflation by the end of the year. This agreement (henceforward referred to as the May Agreement) provides the basis for a $3 billion loan from the IMF under the new Structural Transformation Facility.[1] This paper discusses the prospects for achieving this target and the more ambitious target of a stable, convertible exchange rate. The discussion is based on the analytical work carried out by the author and his associates at the Macroeconomic and Finance Unit of the Ministry of Finance.

The proximate cause of the high inflation is clear. As shown in Figure 3.1, and well known to the Russian reformers, monthly inflation has tended to follow monthly increases in the money supply (M2) with a lag of approximately 3 months. There is little doubt that the growth of the money supply has been the proximate cause of Russia's ongoing high inflation, though the precise timing of month-to-month inflation is also related to the timing of administrative price changes (e.g. for energy,

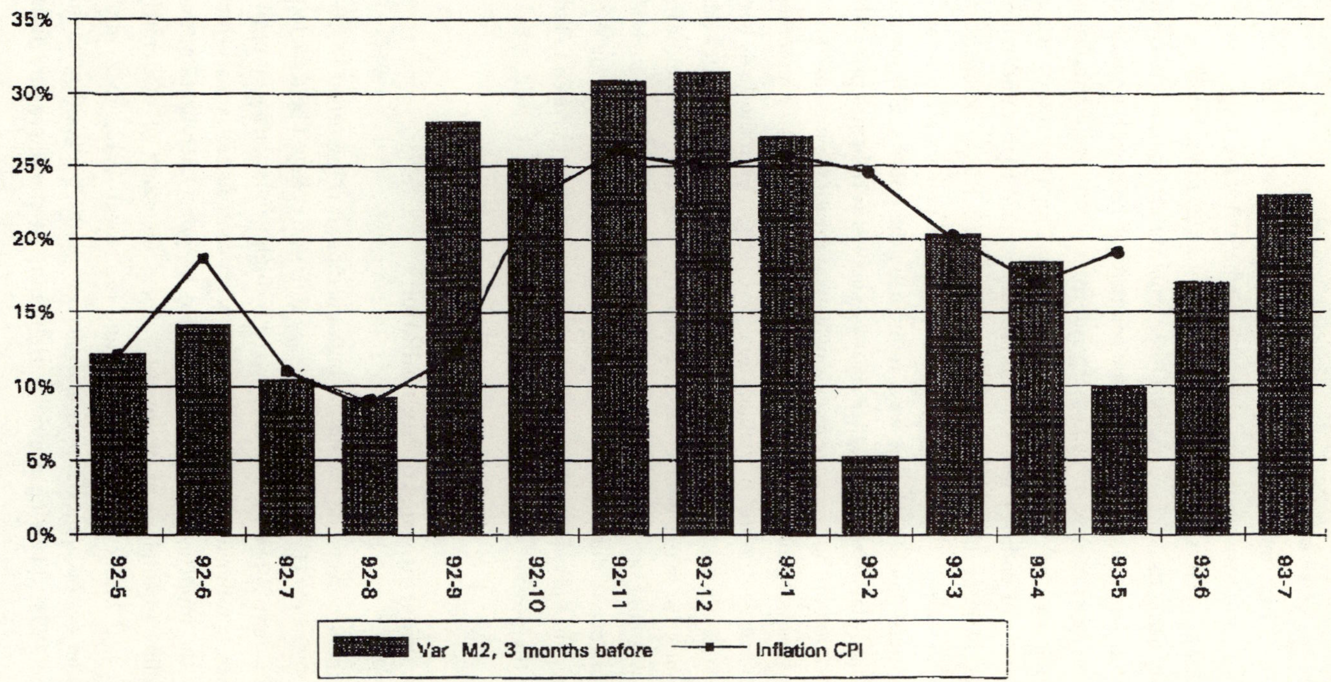


Source: calculations of Jochem Wermuth, Peter Orszag, Jacques Delpla, MFU

**Figure 3.1** Russia 1992–3: monthly inflation (CPI) and growth of the money supply 3 months before

public transport, and utilities). The real problems in slowing inflation thereby revolve around the problems of slowing the growth of the money supply.

As in any case of high inflation, the problems of reducing money growth are economic, political, and institutional in character. Some issues are unique to the former Soviet Union, such as the problem of several countries in the "ruble zone" all simultaneously using the same currency. Other problems are common to countries in transition from socialism, including the countries of Eastern Europe, such as the difficulty of weaning state-owned enterprises from cheap credits. And some problems are emblematic of virtually all countries battling high inflation, such as the political difficulty of ending consumer and producer subsidies that undermine budgetary balance. None of these problems is insurmountable in Russia. Stabilization is within Russia's reach in 1993, if realistic but consistent policies are pursued.

Russia's reformers should seek new ways to intensify the political and institutional forces behind stabilization. In other areas of successful reform – price liberalization, unification of the exchange rate, voucher privatization – bold executive actions were taken rapidly, often in the face of strong initial opposition which then diminished over time. In the area of stabilization, by contrast, even the goals have typically been stated in gradual terms (for example, the May agreement states that "Our ultimate objective is to stabilize the exchange rate" but that "in the meantime, the ruble will continue to float. . ."). International experience and Russia's own recent experience strongly suggest that a bold package of actions should be undertaken to peg the currency and bring the high inflation to a decisive end. This paper discusses the possible contours of such a package.

## The economic underpinnings of high inflation

To understand the prospects for ending the high inflation, it is important to have clearly in mind the recent chronology of monetary and fiscal policy. There are four phases to keep in view: 1) pre-1992, characterized by highly inflationary monetary and fiscal policies, combined with administrative price controls; 2) January-June 1992, in which the monetary overhang was ended by price liberalization, and inflation was falling to single-digit-per-month rates as the result of moderately restrictive CBR and budgetary policies; 3) June-December 1992, involving a strong acceleration of the money supply and increase of the budget deficit; and 4) January–June 1993, involving a modest tightening of monetary and fiscal policies, with the announced intention to tighten further throughout 1993. Even in the fourth phase, however, the budget deficit remains large, especially as a result of continuing subsidies on consumer and producer goods. Let us consider each of these phases in turn.

### *Pre-1992 monetary and fiscal policy*

In 1990 and 1991, there was a substantial buildup of excess aggregate demand, leading to intensified shortages and black-market inflation. The Soviet budget deficit was enormous (around 20 percent of GNP in 1991), and was financed by credit creation. The money supply (M2) relative to GNP rose significantly, reaching 85 percent of GNP at the end of 1991.[2] Also, wages rose sharply while prices remained constrained by official price controls, so that the measured real wage shot up far above historical norms. Of course, the real wage could not be converted into real purchasing power given the increasing intensity of shortages at official prices. Monetary policy was gravely complicated by the emergence in 1991 of 15 independent central banks, one in each of the republics, in addition to Gosbank (which was closed only after the dissolution of the Soviet Union in December 1991). Each republican central bank assumed the authority to issue ruble credits without aggregate limits or even rudimentary cooperation. The printing of ruble banknotes remained in the preserve of the Soviet Government and then the Russian Government, though several other republics introduced parallel banknotes, which in most cases eventually became the basis of distinct national currencies.

### *January-May, 1992*

The monetary overhang was eliminated in January 1992 by the liberalization and resulting large jump in prices, estimated at 245 percent in the month. During February-June 1992, monetary and fiscal policies were moderately restrictive (at least in comparison with the preceding price jump), with M2 growing at an average of 10 percent per month, in the face of much larger price increases following liberalization. Monthly inflation rates fell to around 10 percent by mid-year, reaching the low point of 9 percent in August 1992.

*June-December, 1992*

The increasing tightening of monetary and fiscal conditions prompted both political and economic reactions. The industrial and agricultural lobbies pressed for increased credits, as did the other states in the ruble zone. Many of the CIS states, most importantly Ukraine, introduced substitutes for ruble banknotes (even before formally creating a new currency), thereby increasing the cash money supply in the remaining part of the ruble area. Large inter-enterprise arrears appeared, adding to the pressures for new credit increases. These pressures led to a change in Central Bank leadership, with Victor Gerashchenko replacing Georgii Matyukhin. The new CBR leadership sharply increased the growth of the money supply, to around 30 percent per month on average during July-December. Various budgetary subsidies, and especially implicit subsidies on imported items (in the so-called centralized imports scheme, discussed below), were large and rising.

*January-June, 1993*

The acceleration of the money supply led to near-hyperinflationary conditions by the end of 1992, with inflation rising from its low in August to 27 percent in December, with a clear upward trend. After the change in Government in December 1992, the new cabinet declared the intention to avert hyperinflation by tightening macroeconomic conditions. The money supply growth moderated, and inflation fell to around 20 percent by mid-year. Modest budgetary tightening was pursued, although campaign promises by the President and Supreme Soviet made during the April referendum drive threatened to destabilize fiscal policy. The Government reiterated its intention to tighten fiscal policy in the May agreement with the CBR and the IMF. The agreement established tighter limits on central bank financing of the budget, and a target of monthly inflation of 5 percent by December 1993.

To judge the feasibility of the targets, it is important to gauge more carefully the reasons behind the money supply increases in 1992, as well as the situation with the budget as of mid-1993. Turning first to monetary policy, is the CBR correct to argue that the rapid money supply was inevitable, in effect a "lesser evil" in the face of falling output and rising inter-enterprise arrears? Will similar problems plague the renewed attempt to tighten credit in 1993?

Table 3.1 shows the distribution of CBR credits to the economy in 1992. We see that about half of the credit expansion was destined for industrial enterprises.[3] One-third was destined for budgetary financing, and fully one-fourth was destined for other republics. Since total credits were about 40 percent of Russian GNP in 1992, around 10 percent of GNP actually was lent (in effect given) to the neighboring states. Let us turn first to consider the CBR's motivations for the large expansion of credit to industry, and then consider the credits to the "ruble zone" and to the budget.

**Table 3.1** Central Bank credits in 1992 (bn rubles)

| | Total increase | | Percent of GDP |
|---|---|---|---|
| | (rubles) | (percent) | |
| Total | 6,099 | 100 | 40 |
| Budget | 1,263 | 21 | 8 |
| Enterprises: | 3,306 | 54 | 22 |
| via banks | 2,524 | 41 | 16 |
| via Ministry of Finance | 782 | 13 | 6 |
| Other republics | 1,532 | 25 | 10 |

*Note*: credits to enterprises includes all central bank credits to commercial banks, plus several credit lines via the Ministry of Finance, including credits for working capital indexation (600 billion rubles), and various sectoral loans. There are several off-budget governmental accounts that ran surpluses in 1992, so that net central bank credit to the consolidated government sector is less than shown.

## Credits to the enterprise sector

The Central Bank (and parts of the Russian Government opposed to restrictive monetary policy) gave several reasons for the inflationary financing of industry in 1992. In mid-1992, at the start of the acceleration of money growth, CBR Chairman Viktor V. Gerashchenko asserted that the money supply had to "catch up" with the price increases at the start of 1992. Since prices had risen several-fold, while the money supply had been held in check (at least relative to prices), the CBR claimed that real money balances were now inadequate for the productive sector of the economy. The alleged shortage of real money balances was said to be an important factor in the falling production and in the rise of inter-enterprise arrears. In fact, the Central Bank argued explicitly that it would be possible to increase production and reduce arrears by increasing the money supply, without an increase in inflation.

The CBR also maintained that, in any event, price stabilization was premature since Russian enterprises and the Russian Government were not yet equipped to deal with a truly competitive economic environment, complete with bankruptcies and high unemployment. According to the CBR, enterprises should first be given time to raise their efficiency through increased investments, in order to lower the eventual costs of stabilization. Moreover, the CBR maintained that Russia was unequipped to handle rising unemployment, so that it had no choice but to maintain rapid credit growth to preserve jobs.

These positions have in fact been widely held among Russian political elites and state managers. They reflect various confusions that have hindered adequate monetary policies. The first confusion is that money should have "caught up" with prices after the price liberalization at the start of 1992. Russia began the price liberalization in a condition of extreme excess demand and shortages, so that the average market-clearing price level was much higher than the official price level for the level of the money supply in the economy as of January 1992. It was therefore to be expected (as had occurred in Poland, for example), that price liberalization would not only change relative prices, but would raise the average price level, even with no further changes in the money supply. In other words, it was to be expected that prices would rise sharply relative to the money supply. Once macroeconomic balance was reestablished after the jump in prices following price liberalization, *further* money supply increases should have been expected to raise prices yet again. This is of course what happened.

The second mistake was to view the decline in industrial production as a result of monetary policy, rather than structural adjustment. One of the striking lessons of Eastern Europe's adjustment has been that *every* country in the region has experienced a sharp initial drop in production irrespective of the tightness or looseness of monetary policy, as shown in Table 3.2. In fact, the "shock therapy" of Poland has resulted in the smallest drop of production, while the supposed "gradualist" cases of Bulgaria and Romania have had far larger drops.[4] In the FSU, Ukraine's highly inflationary policies have certainly not saved Ukraine's industrial sector from large decline. Evidently, something is going on much deeper than monetary policy. The socialist economies were heavily distorted in the sectoral distribution of resources and output, with heavy industry built up at the expense of light industry and services. In the Soviet Union, the buildup was concentrated especially in the military-industrial sector. After price liberalization and a sharp cutback in state orders in each of the economies in transition, the heavy industry simply lacks customers. Even with cheap credits to maintain production, the enterprises cannot find customers to buy the output.[5]

**Table 3.2** Industrial production in Eastern Europe, 1989–92 (change in %)

| | 1990 | 1991 | 1992 | 1989–92 (cumulative change) |
|---|---|---|---|---|
| Poland | -24.2 | -11.9 | +3.5 | -30.1 |
| Bulgaria | -12.6 | -23.3 | -15.0 | -43.0 |
| Czechoslovakia | -3.5 | -21.2 | -10.6 | -32.0 |
| Hungary | -4.5 | -19.1 | -9.8 | -30.3 |
| Romania | -19.0 | -22.7 | -22.0 | -51.2 |

*Source*: United Nations, Economic Commission for Europe, *Economic Bulletin for Europe*, 1992.

The third error was to view the inter-enterprise arrears as a sign of overly tight monetary policy. In fact, several related characteristics of the Russian economy seem to have contributed to the problem, as stressed by Jacek Rostowski and others: 1) enterprises were not used to demanding payment from their customers, since they had previously been guaranteed payments by the state following shipments according to the state-order system; 2) enterprises expected that the CBR or the Government would continue to guarantee such payments; 3) there were virtually no penalties for late payments; 4) enterprises continued to ship to customers even when they *knew* that the customer could not pay, because of their expectation of a bailout combined with a lack of alternative customers in any case; 5) the breakdown of the settlements process among the banks, including very long delays in the clearing of payments, led to unpredictability in receipt of payments and a spread of illiquidity even to otherwise healthy enterprises; and 6) standard payments mechanisms such as letters of credit, to guarantee the customer's ability to pay his bills, were underdeveloped or completely non-existent. These issues needed to be addressed directly, not through a return to inflationary financing, which simply added to the high costs of transactions in the economy.

The fourth error was to believe that inflationary financing would actually spur investments and structural change in the economy. Of course, the CBR's view of structural change was enormously constricted, as it viewed the economy almost entirely from the vantage point of the *existing state firms*. It had no conception that expansionary credits to these enterprises actually denied resources to the competing private enterprises trying to get established. It believed that adjustment could and should take place only through existing firms privileged with access to the CBR credits. Moreover, the CBR failed to understand that real adjustment within the enterprises would take place only after a hard budget constraint pressed the enterprises to make changes, and only after a stable monetary environment created the conditions for long-term financing and meaningful long-term expectations.

The irony is that the high-inflation policies of the central bank probably did more to damage the enterprise sector than to help, even putting aside the damage imposed indirectly on the rest of the economy by the inflation tax and the instability in the society. In total, the enterprises received about 20 percent of GNP in credits from the banking system in 1992, but the enterprises also had to build up increased bank balances throughout the year in order to offset the effects of inflation on the enterprises' own working capital. Thus, the net addition to ruble bank balances by enterprises was on the order of 10 percent of GNP, while the increase in dollar balances held in Russian banks was approximately 6–8 percent of GNP (not to mention the billions built up in foreign banks as a result of hidden capital flight). Overall, the enterprise sector used most of the credits merely to build money balances, rather than to fund production or restructuring. The inflationary financing was, to a significant extent, like a dog chasing its own tail: enterprises were loaned money by the CBR and the Ministry of Finance to replenish working capital that was being depleted by the inflation tax!

But as we have stressed, the overall effect was hardly benign. The high inflation lowered the capital flight and a drop in investment by both Russian and foreign investors. The high inflation stifled the development of a long-term capital market. Bank loans are almost entirely less than one year, and overwhelmingly three months or less, as a result of the highly unpredictable monetary environment. The combination of high inflation and slow settlements on inter-enterprise payments further undermined normal business life. Since payments were routinely delayed by as much as one month, the real value of payments could easily vary by 25 percent as a result of the unpredictability of the payments process. In sum, the high inflation sapped the strength of the supply response of the economy, by raising transactions costs, imposing a high inflation-tax on enterprises, encouraging capital flight, and undermining the development of a long-term financial market.

The final error was to believe that the cheap credits were an effective "jobs program" for the economy, and therefore necessary to avoid high unemployment. The economics are rather straightforward. Labour costs are a small proportion of total costs of production, perhaps 20 percent in the military-industrial sector. It is vastly more efficient to subsidize job losers through unemployment compensation than it is to maintain production of unwanted products. Moreover, the Government had established already in 1992 a Federal Employment Service (FES) to provide unemployment benefits. The institutional mechanisms were being set in place. It is of course vital to fund the FES adequately, and it will be much easier to do so with a cutback in other CBR credits.

## The ruble zone

The Russian Government and the CBR failed to come to grips with the problem of the ruble area in 1992. Ironically, part of the difficulty lay in encouragement from the IMF and the EC to maintain a ruble zone despite the obvious inability of the participating countries to manage such a zone in a responsible, non-inflationary manner. The IMF and EC views were not the decisive factors, but they gave confidence to politicians in the CIS that wanted to maintain the ruble area for other reasons. The result was a substantial inflationary impulse that was probably even more important in fact than its one-fourth share of total credit expansion shown in Table 3.1.[6]

The economic problem of the ruble area at the start of 1992 should have been clear. Fifteen central banks were simultaneously issuing ruble credits to the governments and commercial banks of the respective states. No single central bank outside of Russia had the incentive to maintain tight monetary policies in the face of this collective non-system. Nor were there any real prospects for active coordination in an environment of great pressures within each state for inflationary finance and no institutional mechanisms for enforcement of monetary rules across the fifteen states. In fact, on the grounds of trade, public finance, politics, and labour mobility, there was simply no reason to suppose that the FSU constituted an optimal currency area, and in fact every reason to believe the contrary. The strong logic of the situation suggests that each of the new sovereign states should manage their own national money, and that these distinct currencies should trade freely against each other with floating exchange rates.[7]

Unfortunately, despite many CIS meetings and supposed deadlines for action (including mid-1992 and end-1992), there was little orderly progress on these problems. Russia failed to adopt a coherent strategy. A few states adopted their own currencies, while others issued currency notes alongside ruble bank deposits, thereby subjecting Russia to a significant inflow of banknotes, (incidentally, without a murmur from the IMF). In June 1992, the CBR created the foundation for a distinct Russian bank ruble, by ending the automatic clearing of bank deposits in other republics into bank deposits in Russian banks. Up until June, a Kazakhstan enterprise could automatically pay a Russian enterprise with rubles held in a Kazakhstan commercial bank. After June, the Kazakhstan rubles would be settled in Russian rubles only if the Central Bank of Kazakhstan (CBK) held adequate deposits at the CBR, or if the CBR explicitly granted the CBK credit or an overdraft for the settlement.

To be specific, the Kazakhstan enterprise would transfer rubles to the CBK; the CBK would transfer rubles to the CBR, assuming that it held adequate balances; and the CBR would credit the account of the Russian enterprise. If the CBK did not hold adequate balances (and could not get an overdraft from the CBR), then the transaction would not be cleared. Alternatively, the Kazakhstan enterprise could simply hold a ruble account in a Russian bank, and then use the Russian bank balance directly to make the payment to the Russian enterprise.

The new CBR policy had one advantage; other republics could no longer *automatically* issue ruble credits for use in purchasing Russian goods. But it was also seriously deficient, since it left the ruble area with an ostensible common currency that in fact was composed of distinct and mutually inconvertible national currencies! Even if the Kazakhstan enterprise held adequate ruble deposits, there was no guarantee that it could use them to buy Russian goods. In fact, if Kazakhstan as a whole was in deficit to Russia (as evidenced by a negative CBK balance at the CBR), then the Kazakhstan enterprise could not rely on using its domestic bank balances for a purchase in Russia.

One important step was taken towards the solution of the ruble area problem by the June action of the CBR, and another by the withdrawal of Ukraine and the Baltic states from the ruble area in the summer and fall of 1992. Nonetheless, the problem continued in another guise in mid-1992, when Russia began issuing large amounts of new credits (essentially overdraft facilities) to the other republics, including Ukraine, in order to maintain their purchases of Russian goods. This policy resulted from a powerful alliance of the industrial lobby with the Russian foreign policy community interested in smooth relations with the neighbours. The result was that, in fact, Kazakhstan and the other CIS states never really ran out of rubles at the CBR: their accounts were continuously, and almost automatically, replenished.

The pressures for credits were most readily fulfilled for the countries that stayed in the ruble area. Credits to Ukraine and the Baltic states have been sharply curtailed in 1993 (though Ukraine continues to receive credit in the form of late, or non, payments for oil and gas shipments). For the states still in the ruble area, a shortage of credits leads automatically to inconvertibility of one ruble to another, and this makes it extremely difficult for the CBR and the Russian Government to resist demands for new credits. If new currencies were introduced by these states, then convertibility could be maintained by the fluctuations in the market exchange rate between these currencies and the Russian ruble.

To this date, there has been no definitive solution to the ruble area, even though more and more of the CIS states are leaving on their own accord. Certain Central Asian states, particularly Kazakhstan and Uzbekistan, want to remain inside the ruble area, almost surely because they recognize that this is the clearest route to the continued flow of cheap credits. Russia has set more stringent targets for providing credit to the other republics, but in fact only separate national currencies will overcome the problem of currency inconvertibility. We return to this issue below.

## Fiscal policy and inflationary finance

In addition to CBR loans to enterprises and to the CIS states, credits to finance the budget deficit are the third major source of inflationary pressure in the economy. In 1992, CBR financing of the general government was approximately 8 percent of GNP. The overall government budget deficit was approximately 20 percent of GNP, with the balance (12 percent of GNP) representing subsidies on imported items financed by external sources. (The exact nature of these subsidies is described later.)

All countries in transition face severe fiscal problems, as government budgets are caught between declining tax collections from the state-enterprise sector, combined with rising social demands. Russia's fiscal crisis is compounded by the political weakness of the federal government in the face of rising demands from Russia's 88 regional governments. The regions have been able to secure massive tax exemptions, particularly from export and raw materials taxes, as well as special transfers, both of which have seriously weakened the federal budget. On top of this are serious administrative problems in tax collection and enforcement.

Nonetheless, Russia's fiscal problems could be substantially meliorated in straightforward ways. The main source of Russia's ongoing fiscal crisis lies in extensive price controls with various direct and indirect budgetary costs. Elimination of these price controls would also end Russia's budgetary crisis, or at least reduce it to levels consistent with the low inflation rates achieved in Eastern Europe. In this sense, Russia's continuing inflation is characteristic of the high inflation experiences of the populistic episodes in Latin America, where misguided governments attempted to provide "cheap goods" to the public via budget subsidies, and ended up imposing much heavier costs on the public in the form of a burdensome inflation tax.

The major continuing price controls are in the following areas:

1. grain prices, which are held at approximately 30 percent of world levels;
2. energy prices, which vary between 5 percent (for coal and gas) and 20 percent (for oil) of world levels;
3. other import items subject to import subsidies;
4. infrastructure prices (internal transport, communications, housing rents, utilities prices);
5. general profitability margins for some sectors and for firms deemed (rather arbitrarily) to be monopolies.

In all of these areas, the government attempts to provide low prices to the population or to other enterprises that use the subsidized or controlled commodities as inputs, and then ends up paying a heavy budgetary cost to sustain the low prices. In the case of grain, for example, domestic grain prices are held at about 30 percent of world prices through a system of import subsidies for wheat, as well as direct subsidies to producers at various production stages (e.g. cheap energy inputs for state farms, and substantial subsidized credits that are, in effect, grants given the high rate of inflation). As a result of these actions, a loaf of bread in Moscow in June 1993 costs approximately 3.7 U.S. cents. The budgetary costs of these subsidies is probably around $3 billion, or roughly 3 percent of GNP.

Enormous direct and indirect subsidies exist for coal, gas, and oil. In the case of coal, price controls are combined with direct subsidies to coal enterprises, in an amount estimated at 1.5 trillion rubles in 1993, approximately 1.5 percent of GNP. The domestic price of coal in June 1993 is $1 per metric ton, or approximately 3.4 percent of the world price. For gas, domestic prices are simply regulated by the government, and as of June 1993 are set at approximately 5 percent of the world price. In the case of oil, domestic oil prices are kept at around 20 percent of world prices through a system of export quotas. Later on, we will provide estimates of the increase in budgetary revenues that could be achieved by a move towards world prices in energy.

Various import items are also subject to budgetary subsidization, through a system known as "centralized imports". In this arrangement, the government imports a commodity using an international line of credit (e.g. a three-year U.S. credit to import grain). The commodity is then sold to domestic trading companies, typically at a small fraction of the world price. The trading company then markets it on the domestic market. In many cases, such as for sugar, tea, dry milk, meat products, and cocoa, the government actually sells the commodity to the trading company at a price even below the *domestic* market price. The trading company then earns a pure rent by buying the commodity from the government and reselling it in the domestic market. This rent, clearly, is a pure transfer from the budget, without benefit to final consumers. The overall budgetary subsidy under the centralized import system was around $10–12 billion in 1992, and is targeted to be $4–5 billion during 1993. The direct annual costs of the pure rent component are approximately one-third of the total subsidy.

In addition to the various subsidy schemes, the government budget also loses large amounts of revenues as a result of the policy of setting export barriers in the form of administratively distributed quotas, rather than auctioned quota rights or export taxes. Export quotas exist on energy, base metals, various wood products, and some chemical products. Estimates of the budgetary consequences of completely converting the export quotas on energy to export taxes suggest that the revenue gains would be as much as 8 percent of GNP. The MFU does not yet have estimates for most of the other commodities. In the recent agreement between the Government and the CBR on the direction of economic policy, the Government announced the intention to eliminate all non-energy export quotas by end-1993, and to phase out the energy export quotas by end-1994.

Progress has been promised in each of these main fiscal areas in the potentially important May agreement. The main policy commitments include: across-the-board cuts in expenditures; reductions in coal subsidies; increased excise taxes on oil and gas; reductions in grain subsidies; reduction in centralized import subsidies; reduction in interest rate subsidies; and a rather rapid phase-out of export quotas and centralized exports by the government. Nonetheless, even *after* the promised adjustments, the budget deficit remains at around 10 percent of GDP, and there is not yet the intention to stabilize the exchange rate.

## Administrative factors in the high inflation

The inflationary policies should also be understood in the administrative and political context in which the CBR and the Russian Government operated in 1992 and the first part of 1993. Most fundamentally, the Russian Federation emerged from the Soviet Union as a sovereign state only in December 1991, so that the period of economic reform has coincided with a critical and complex period of creating state institutions. This state-building has been characterized by an inadequate constitution carried over from the communist regime, and intense political struggles among rival branches of government, both with the federal and the regional levels, and at times between the federal and regional levels. This struggle has been complicated by the absence of free elections for legislative and executive bodies at the federal, regional, and local levels since the end of the communist regime, thus undermining the clear political legitimacy of the rival governmental institutions.

The specific administrative structures for economic decision making have also been highly inadequate. The dependence of the CBR on the Supreme Soviet is notorious. Not only is there no central bank independence, but the CBR dependence is in fact with the branch of government most hostile to the reforms and to macroeconomic stabilization. But the organizational problems go far deeper.

Until spring 1993, there was virtually no overall macroeconomic policy control or analysis within the Government or the CBR. The Ministry of Finance and the CBR were not seriously engaged in setting or monitoring aggregate credit targets. There were rhetorical bows towards a credit policy, as early as January 1992 when the Central Bank announced that aggregate credit would grow by 15 percent in the first quarter of 1992, a target that was almost immediately exceeded. In practice, the relevant governmental authorities gave far too little attention to overall targets, and made little effort to monitor or fulfil them. As I have stressed many times, part of the problem was the absence of a meaningful offer of Western foreign assistance during 1992. To paraphrase the old Russian joke, the relationship of Russia and the West in the first year of reform was "you pretend to aid us, and we pretend to stabilize". (Of course, the Gaidar-led reforms in 1992 made historic and often spectacular progress in areas other than stabilization, including privatization, liberalization, and creation of public and private market-based institutions).

Many of the basic procedures for crediting and budgeting were carried out without attention to their macroeconomic consequences. Credits to the other republics were routinely approved by the CBR without much governmental scrutiny. Similarly, credits to commercial banks from the CBR were granted without overall macroeconomic targeting or limits. There have been widespread media reports of kickbacks on CBR credits to commercial banks and other republics. Until the spring of 1993, individual ministers, key members of Parliamentary commissions, powerful industrial enterprises, and influential regional authorities, all have had substantial sway on credit policy without any overall macroeconomic constraints. Only with the emergence of the operations of the Credit Commission is there the prospect of limiting credits to meaningful macroeconomic guidelines.

The situation has been greatly complicated by the Presidential authority to issue decrees. While this power has very often been beneficial to the reforms by speeding the process of executive action, it has also been frequently the source of increased deficits. The President has routinely granted tax exemptions to and subsidized credits to key regions and sectors. Also Presidential decrees on price controls have been issued without regard to their budgetary or macroeconomic consequences.

Various other aspects of governmental policy – centralized imports, debt servicing, export quotas, energy pricing, Russian sovereign guarantees given on loans to Russian enterprises – have been made by various committees within the Governmental structure without macroeconomic oversight or considerations of the effects on the budget and money supply. Thus, the Russian Government distributed several billion dollars of foreign credits in 1992 through the centralized import scheme without regard to the enormously serious macroeconomic consequences of the policy.

The situation has begun to improve in 1993, with the activation of the Government Commission on Credit Policy, under the prodding and chairmanship of Deputy Prime Minister Boris Fedorov. The CBR and relevant ministries (among others, the ministries of economy, privatization, foreign economic relations, and the state committee on CIS relations) are represented on the commission. Since

April, the credit commission has been establishing monetary and credit targets for overall macroeconomic policy. A breakthrough occurred in late April when the Government and the CBR negotiated a program of credit limits for the second quarter of 1993. The following month, these credit limits became the basis of the May agreement. The readiness and ability of the Government and the CBR to live within these credit targets will be tested during the remainder of 1993.

## Achieving macroeconomic stabilization

It is evident that there are several important factors involved in the ongoing high inflation in Russia. Pressures for large credits to enterprises continue to arise from concerns over declines in production and rising unemployment, as well as the intensive lobbying by politically powerful industrial enterprises. Pressures to maintain the ruble area, and the accompanying subsidies to the other republics, emanate from domestic exporters as well as foreign policy leaders. Nonetheless, these subsidies have been cut sharply compared with 1992. Credits to the budget overwhelmingly reflect misguided attempts to provide "cheap" goods to the public through subsidy schemes that indirectly tax the public via inflation. All of these pressures are exacerbated by inadequate administrative and political institutions, and widespread inexperience with monetary policy.

Can these pressures be overcome to achieve effective stabilization along the lines that the Government and CBR announced in May 1993? The answer, I strongly believe, is yes. Despite all of the difficulties, Russia is actually closer to stabilization than is commonly believed (the same was true of Poland, Estonia, and several other countries in transition that have succeeded in ending high inflations in recent years). Stabilization can be achieved by a limited number of actions, all administratively feasible, though no doubt politically controversial. These actions would have a very good chance of slowing inflation to low single-digit levels if carried out consistently and vigorously.

Many of the needed actions have already been started in the May agreement. In each area, I believe that stronger actions should now be taken to make a decisive breakthrough on stabilization. I will summarize the main directions of changes that are needed, in my view, to achieve a success in stabilization.

1. *End of the Ruble Area.* The May agreement calls for a significant cutback in credit to the other CIS states, and new procedures to put these credits through

the regular budgetary mechanism. In my view the Government should go further, by explicitly ending the quest for a ruble area, and delinking from the other CIS states. This should be done in a firm, though non-confrontational way, as suggested in Appendix A.

2. *Tighter administrative control on budgeting and crediting.* All budgetary and credit measures proposed within the Government, or in discussions between the Government and the Parliament, or by Presidential decree, should be referred to the Credit Commission for vetting, to determine whether the expenditure proposals are within the macroeconomic limits established by the Government and the CBR.
3. *End of subsidized credits on imports for all goods except grain.* The May agreement calls for a cutback in centralized imports. The policy should be fortified, by eliminating forthwith all centralized import subsidies other than for grain and fodder, particularly since a large part of the non-grain import subsidies constitute a pure rent to state trading organizations.
4. *Raise grain prices to around 50 percent of world levels.* The May agreement calls for a partial cut in grain subsidies, but again the measures can and should go further. Higher grain prices should be passed through into final prices of bread and other foodstuffs, and the extensive subsidies to the grain producing sector should be cut commensurately.
5. *Raise energy prices substantially.* The May agreement calls for modest cuts in energy subsidies (particularly to the coal sector), and modest increases in prices. Energy prices should be increased more sharply, through a combination of excise taxes, price decontrol, and increased exports of coal and oil. Special social groups (e.g. schools, hospitals, etc.) should be partially compensated to cushion the higher energy prices. The specific recommendations are contained in Appendix B, and are designed to raise at least 5 percent of GNP, net of the subsidies for social groups.
6. *Peg the exchange rate in conjunction with these actions.* The May agreement calls for a continuation of a floating exchange rate, "until financial policies have been tightened and inflation has been substantially reduced". However, as in virtually every successful stabilization in the past decade, a pegged exchange rate at the *start* of stabilization would provide a crucial "nominal anchor" to the stabilization process, not only through its direct effects on the goods market prices, but also through its disciplining effect on the Government's and CBR's macroeconomic policies.

7. *Fiscal federalism.* The central government can reduce some of the fiscal burdens arising from social spending by giving increased responsibility to regional and local governments, combined with increased authority at the regional and local levels to establish independent tax regimes. Currently, the Federal government sets all tax rates, and shares revenues with the region. The Federal Government should instead reserve particular taxes to itself (personal and corporate income tax; trade taxes; VAT; and national excise taxes, e.g. on energy), and then permit the regions to establish independent taxes on income, sales, property, and royalties.
8. *Mobilization of international financial support.* At the G-7 ministerial meeting in Tokyo in April, the leading industrial countries committed $28 billion in international resources to Russia for 1993. This sum may be augmented at the Tokyo Summit in July with an additional $4 billion Privatization Fund, supported by the U.S. Government, and designed for use by newly-privatized enterprises for restructuring and by oblasts burdened with increased social costs as a result of restructuring. The key point of international assistance is that it can directly substitute for CBR financing to the government, the enterprises, and the other republics. Each $1 of financing of the budget, for example, directly reduces the CBR financing by 1,100 rubles.

The May agreement provides an excellent starting point for a real and decisive stabilization. According to the benchmark data, agreed to with the IMF in May, the overall budget deficit for 1993 (after the measures agreed to in the May package) is targeted at 10 percent of GDP, of which 6.9 percent is to be foreign financed (mainly through commodity credits) and 3.0 is to be domestically financed. In fact, the gross domestic financing is 6.1 percent of GDP, combined with a scheduled net repayment of internal debt of around 3 percent of GDP. The internal debt repayment involves so-called internal "commodity loans" in which the Soviet government promised subsidized automobiles to certain groups. Honouring these commitments in 1993 would now cost around 3 percent of GDP. For purposes of increased clarity, let us consider the IMF-agreed baseline in the following terms:

| | % of GDP |
|---|---|
| Total to be financed: | |
| deficit | 10.0 |
| commodity loan amortization | 3.0 |
| Financing: | |
| domestic | 6.0 |
| foreign | 7.0 |

Now consider some adjustments to the baseline. First, the domestic commodity loans can likely be stretched out or even formally rescheduled over a number of years, rather than paid out this year. I would assume that at least 2.5 percent of GDP of the commodity loan amortization can be postponed this year.

Second, foreign financing can be increased by at least $2.0 billion, or 2.0 percent of GDP, compared to the IMF baseline, with the adoption of an IMF standby agreement (not counted in the baseline) and a second World Bank rehabilitation loan.

Third, the IMF baseline probably overstates by at least $0.5 billion (0.5 percent of GDP) the amount that will be paid on foreign debt service during 1993, in view of the substantial amount of negotiations that have yet to reach agreements with the various creditors.

Fourth, further steps on energy prices, compared with those announced in the May agreement, should recoup an additional 3.5 percent of GDP. Note that the May agreement calls for a 1.6 percent of GDP increase in net revenues as a result of energy measures (cuts in coal subsidies and higher excises on oil and gas), while Appendix B specifies an adjustment of at least 5 percent of GDP.

Fifth, further cuts in centralized imports could likely net another 1.5 percent of GDP in budgetary savings.

Sixth, further cuts in grain subsidies could likely net at least 0.5 percent of GDP, and probably twice that amount.

Adding up all of these further adjustments, we have additional budgetary savings or foreign financing of around 10.5 percent of GDP. Note that this would more than permit a *complete elimination of CBR financing of the budget deficit* according to the May baseline. Even if the baseline is too optimistic in certain areas, it is clear that the domestic financing by the CBR could be virtually eliminated.

Note that the pegging of the ruble exchange rate would not require a complete elimination of CBR financing. It is likely that the combination of administered price changes on energy and grains, inflationary inertia, and necessary real appreciation of the ruble would all mean that inflation will continue at a rate of a few percent per month (perhaps 3–5 percent per month) even after the exchange rate is stabilized. This continued modest inflation permits an increase in the nominal ruble money supply, which in turn allows for a limited amount of CBR financing of the budget.

## The political base for monetary stabilization

The biggest potential obstacle to stabilization in Russia today is that the executive branch, including the President and the Government, might not have the political will to stand behind a rigorous stabilization program. In 1992, the obstacles were far more pervasive, including a renegade central bank, the active opposition of the Supreme Soviet, an uncontrolled ruble zone, and the lack of an overall monetary framework for government policy. The situation is vastly more favourable today, since the CBR is more or less in compliance with Government policies; the Supreme Soviet is greatly weakened as an opposition force; the ruble zone has been largely abandoned and could be eliminated completely in short order; and the Credit Commission has the de facto mandate to establish overall macroeconomic targets for the Government and the CBR.

Nonetheless, the Government itself remains divided between those who would go slowly and those who would act decisively now. The gradualists believe that stabilization is politically damaging, and thus must be pursued at the right moment, presumably after a new and supportive Parliament is elected. This idea is doubly wrong in my view. First, stabilization need not be politically damaging, at least not in an electoral sense. The public strongly desires an end to high inflation, and most of the stabilizing measures affect special interests rather than the broad population. Even though unemployment will rise with tight macroeconomic policies, the unemployment will affect only a small proportion of the labour force, while all social groups will benefit from the stabilization of the currency.

Second, there is likely to be no more fortuitous moment than the present to make the decisive breakthrough. The executive branch is unhampered by a *legitimate* parliamentary opposition, and CBR opposition has been checked. Also, summertime is traditionally the most favourable time to raise energy prices. It would be a mistake to squander the current moment on the hope that the future is even more amenable to strong stabilization measures.

Even the administrative and political disarray of the government could be overcome by a vigorous push of policies by the main reformers. History shows that successful stabilizations are made by a few individuals, typically over the vociferous objections of their political colleagues.[8] Stabilizations therefore almost always require a *package* of measures, since the reformers must push through a number of controversial actions at once to have a chance of success. Piecemeal actions may be enough to forestall hyperinflation, but are rarely sufficient to win the psychological confidence of the people. The package of measures strongly raises the credibility of the government with the population, and raises the power of the stabilizers within the government by committing the government in a bold and explicit way to a program of action.

## Appendix A Suggested Russian policy on currencies in the CIS

### *I. Overview*

1. The current policy of trying to preserve the ruble area has been an expensive failure. Monetary policy is not under adequate control and payments problems on interstate trade have not been solved. A true currency area would require a single central bank, as opposed to a separate central bank in each CIS state. The CIS states are not willing to eliminate their central banks and to cede their sovereign control over monetary policy to a new centralized institution, and even if they were, the Russian Government lacks the political and administrative will to monitor banks and control monetary policy in other states. The only solution is the introduction of a separate national currency in each CIS state.
2. There are very high costs of any further delay in introducing separate currencies. In fact, the rubles of the various republics are already effectively separate currencies that have black-market exchange rates between them (the "Kazakhstan ruble", for example, trades at a discount vis-à-vis the "Russian ruble"). Nonetheless, there are no legal foreign exchange markets for the free exchange of these currencies, so that rubles of the various republics are de facto inconvertible. This accelerates the breakdown of trade among the republics. Contrary to some opinions, trade among the CIS states would be greatly strengthened, not reduced, by the swift introduction of national currencies in each of the CIS states.

### *II. Policy actions*

3. The Russian Government should explicitly declare the end of the attempt to create a single ruble area. Russia should seek to strengthen economic links within the CIS according to normal market conditions based on separate national

currencies in each of the republics. Separate national currencies will provide a key step towards macroeconomic stability within the CIS, and towards market-based trade within the CIS.

4. The Russian Government should call on each CIS state to establish the juridical basis of a separate national currency before July 1, and to begin operation of a separate national currency on or before July 1. Until then, the Russian Federation should treat ruble bank deposits in other CIS states as separate national currencies of those states (e.g. Kazakhstan rubles, Uzbekistan rubles, etc.). Each state should prepare for the replacement of ruble banknotes by banknotes of the new currency by no later than October 1. Russian rubles collected by the exchange of banknotes should be returned to the Russian Federation for removal from circulation.
5. The Russian Government should stop all credits (technical credits and inter-state loans) to CIS states that do not introduce their own national currencies. Moreover, the Russian Government should reschedule existing debts of CIS states (e.g. on "technical credits" from 1992) only after the introduction of new national currencies. The Russian Government should consider limited inter-state credits to other CIS states after the introduction of separate national currencies, but only after the introduction of those currencies.
6. The Russian Government and Central Bank should take necessary measures to preserve and strengthen the role of the Russian ruble as a currency for inter-state trade within the CIS. CIS residents and enterprises outside Russia may hold Russian ruble bank accounts in Russian banks, and may use those accounts for payments to Russian enterprises and households, and for participation in the Russian foreign exchange markets (consistent with the foreign exchange regulations of the Russian Federation).
7. The Russian Government and Central Bank should also work closely with cooperating states to encourage the development of foreign exchange markets for converting the new national currencies into Russian rubles and vice versa. Russian commercial banks should be licensed to hold correspondent accounts directly in the commercial banks of other states, while the commercial banks in the other states will be allowed to hold correspondent accounts in Russian banks. These correspondent accounts would provide the basis for the foreign exchange trading among national currencies, without a direct role of the central banks. Naturally, these off-shore correspondent accounts will be subjected to normal prudential requirements.

8. Russia should work closely with the cooperating states to speed up payments. The payments system under the arrangements suggested here would likely be *much faster* since it would be based on correspondent accounts of commercial banks, and would not require clearing through the Russian Central Bank.
9. At least at the inception, national currencies should float freely against the Russian ruble, to ensure convertibility of national currencies into Russian rubles and vice versa. After the establishment of a foreign exchange market, other states may choose to peg the value of their currency to the Russian ruble, and this would be acceptable to Russia assuming that the currency remains freely convertible into rubles.

## Appendix B Suggested energy sector policies for Q3 and Q4, 1993

| | Policy | Revenue gain (as % of GDP) |
|---|---|---|
| 1. | Impose a 22% exise tax on sales of natural gas and increase the state price to R.15,300, approximately 35% of the world price | 1.6 |
| 2. | Subsidize households, hospitals and day-care centres for one-half of the real gas price increase | -1.0 |
| 3. | Rescind the price regulation fund for oil and increase the mean effective oil excise tax to 25% | -0.4 |
| 4a. | *Variant A* Remove all energy export restrictions and raise the export tariff on oil to 50% | 8.1 |
| 5a. | Subsidize vulnerable consumers of oil | -2.0 |
| 6a. | Savings on coal-subsidies after consumer subsidies | 0.0 |
| 7a. | Net revenue gains from policy package A | 6.3 |
| 4b. | *Variant B* Gradually abolish the export quota system and keep the export tariff at 30% | 1.9 |
| 5b. | Auction 4 million tons of oil quotas each month | 3.5 |
| 6b. | Subsidize vulnerable consumers of oil | -1.8 |
| 7b. | Net revenue gain from policy package B | 3.8 |

*Source*: Calculations of Jochen Wermuth, Peter Orszag, Jacques Delpla, MFU

## Notes

* The Macroeconomic and Finance Unit (MFU) of the Russian Government gratefully acknowledges the generous financial support of the Government of Sweden and the Ford Foundation. All views expressed here are my own, and not necessarily those of the Russian Government, or the financial sponsors of the MFU.

1. "Economic Policy Statement of the Government of Russia and Central Bank of Russia," May 1993.
2. For 1991, GNP was estimated at 1130 billion rubles, and end-of-year money supply at 938 billion [Note: a revised estimate will calculate annual GNP at December 1991 prices, rather than year-average prices].
3. These credits came in several ways: CBR credits to commercial banks, onlent to enterprises at market rates; CBR credits to commercial banks onlent to enterprises at subsidized rates to be covered by the budget; and CBR credits lent to the Ministry of Finance for onlending to the enterprises. In the accounting in the table, this last kind of lending is considered as enterprise finance, rather than budgetary finance.
4. Of course, the data are imprecise, so that a careful statement would say that Poland's fall was among the lowest, and that there is no evidence that Poland's tight stabilization measures added to the cumulative decline measured over a three-year period.
5. A particularly graphic case is steel output. Soviet steel production in 1990 was 160 million metric tons, compared with 80 mmt in the U.S., despite a U.S. economy roughly 10 times the size. There is simply no demand for such large amounts of steel, particularly after the drastic cutbacks in tanks, MIGs, submarines, aircraft carriers, and other military output.
6. Part of the enterprise credits were an attempt to replenish enterprise working balances that were depleted by the inflation tax. Thus, if there had been a smaller inflationary impulse coming from the non-enterprise credits (budget and other republics), there would have been fewer credits extended to the enterprises as well. For this reason, the credits to the budget and to the other republics probably account for well more than half of the underlying inflationary impulse in the economy.
7. Another logical possibility would be to subordinate all monetary policy to a single monetary authority under Russian control. Even this alternative should be avoided. Russia does not have the ability to monitor the banking systems of the neighboring states (much less with Russia), nor probably to resist the political entreaties to fund deficit countries within the monetary system. In the end, a single, multi-state authority would have deficient monitoring of the banking system, and would naturally prey on Russia's political weaknesses to provoke excessive credit expansion.
8. This is why stabilization programs are often known by the name of their authors, such as Erhard, Salinas, Balcerowicz, and Klaus.

# 4 Dilemmas of Monetary and Financial Policy in Post-Stabilization Russia

*Jacek Rostowski*

## 1 Introduction

Stabilization of high inflation is hard, not only because the political conditions conducive to such an undertaking are not always present, but also because such stabilizations are "regime changes" par excellence. Relationships between variables which existed before the stabilization are violently changed to quite different ones almost overnight. What is more, the new relationships are initially unknown (particularly as regards their quantitative aspect), and yet economic policy cannot cease until the new relationships have been identified. Stabilization is thus technically as well as politically difficult, and it is likely that as many attempted stabilizations have failed as a result of technical errors as from an unconducive political environment. Certainly, if technical mistakes increase the costs of stabilization they can be expected to undermine whatever political support there is for the policy.

This is why this paper is concerned with such technical problems. I take as given the "acquis" of stabilization programs in Post-Communist Economies (PCEs): the abolition of central planning, price liberalization, convertibility at a unified exchange rate, low trade barriers, moves towards world prices for key raw materials, sharp reductions in subsidies, budget equilibrium and an end to accommodative monetary policy. Instead, I concentrate on a number of monetary and financial problems where it seems less evident just what should be done: the techniques of monetary control (Sections 2 and 3), the choice of the exchange rate (Section 4), bad bank debt (Section 5) and inter-enterprise debt (Section 6).

## 2 The behaviour of the money supply after stabilization

A number of countries which experienced very high inflation followed by stabilization in the 1970s, 1980s and 1990s have exhibited a characteristic pattern of behaviour of the money multiplier: as inflation accelerates, the ratio of reserve money (the monetary base) to one's chosen money aggregate increases – i.e. the money multiplier falls and the proportion of the money supply which consists of central bank liabilities becomes large. Upon stabilization this process is reversed, with the ratio of central bank liabilities to commercial bank liabilities in the composition of the money supply falling, so that the money multiplier increases. Figures 4.1–4.6 show that this typical pattern for the M1 multiplier was exhibited for the periods before and after stabilization by Argentina (June 1985 and July 1989), Brazil (February 1986), Poland (January 1990), Uruguay (October 1978) and Yugoslavia (January 1990). Figures 4.7 and 4.8 show that the domestic M2 money multiplier exhibited the same pattern in Poland (1990) and Yugoslavia (1990). Figures 4.9 and 4.10 show that during the high inflation which began with price liberalization in January 1992, Russia has gone through the first part of this typical pattern, and can therefore be expected to experience the same post-stabilization increase in the money multiplier which occurred in the other examples.[1] A number of recent episodes of very high inflation followed by stabilization have failed to exhibit this pattern: these cases, and possible explanations, are discussed in the Appendix.

Two consequences arise from the increase in the money multiplier after stabilization: first, it becomes harder to conduct short-term monetary policy; second, in PCEs – which suffer from a severe shortage of banking skills – the increase in the real value of commercial bank liabilities is likely to create a "bad debt" overhang, which either adds to the contingent national debt, or increases the instability of the monetary system (as a result of the increase in the ratio of commercial to central bank liabilities in the composition of the money supply). We shall address the first question later in this section and the second in Section 5.

But first let us examine the reasons for the money multiplier's "typical pattern" during high inflation and stabilization. It essentially stems from the decline in the willingness of households and firms to hold bank deposits as the inflation tax increases, with nominal interest rates falling relative to the inflation rate. Thus such a flight from bank deposits will not occur if real deposit interest rates do not fall as a result of the increasing inflation.[2] Fleeing bank deposits, households and firms shift into foreign currency, foreign currency deposits, and in some cases –

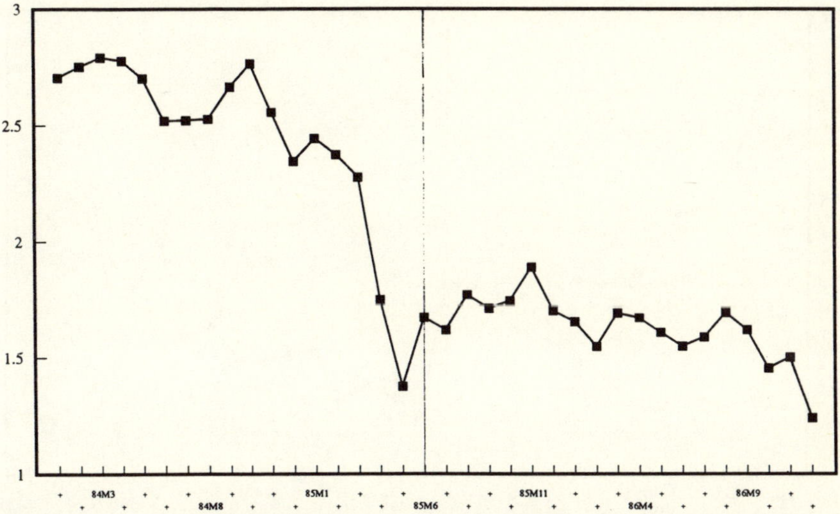


**Figure 4.1** Argentina 1984–6: reserve money to narrow money

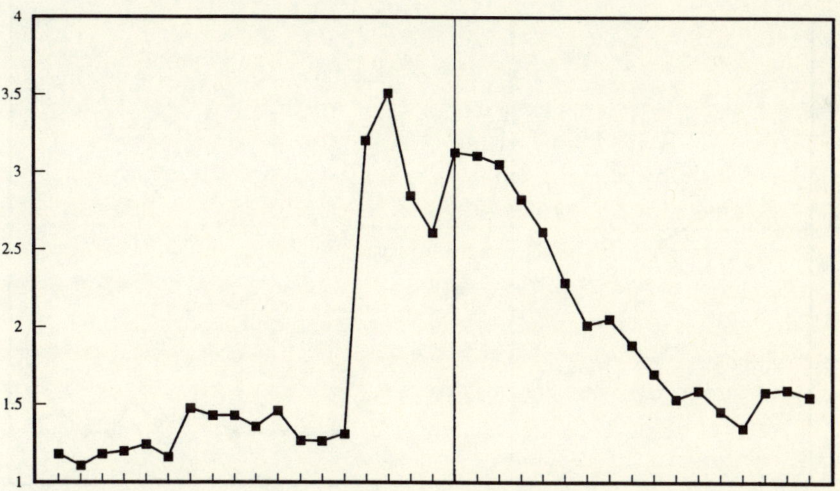


**Figure 4.2** Argentina 1988–90: reserve money to narrow money

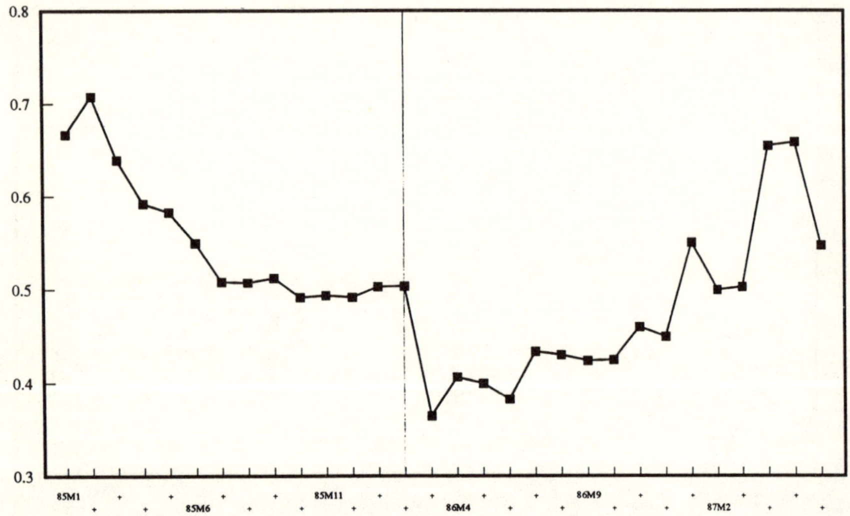


Figure 4.3 Brazil 1985–7: reserve money to narrow money

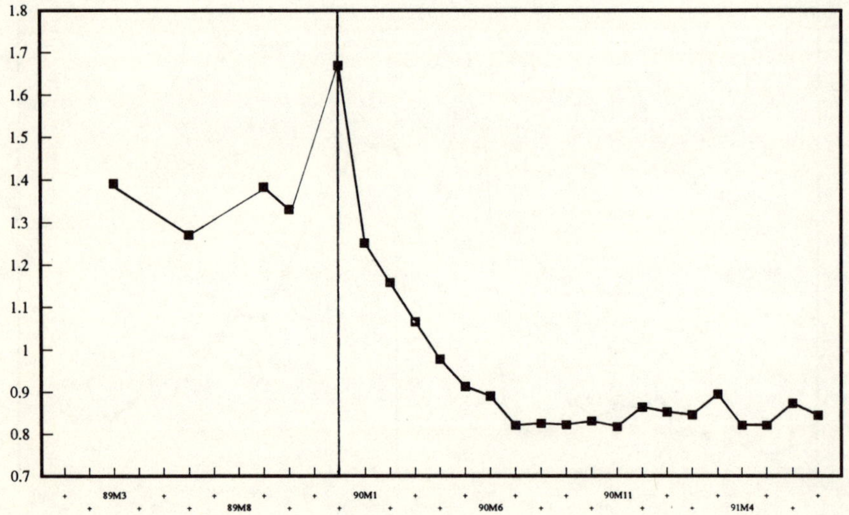


Figure 4.4 Poland 1989–91: reserve money to narrow money

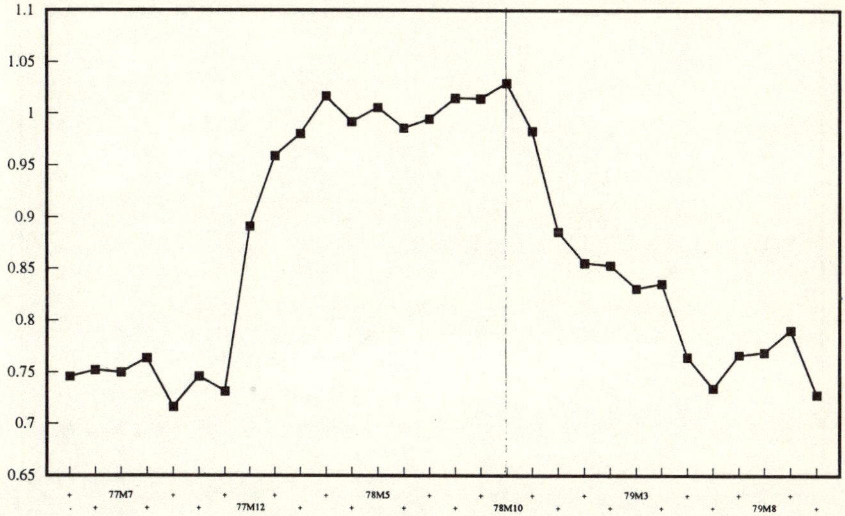


**Figure 4.5** Uruguay 1977–9: reserve money to narrow money

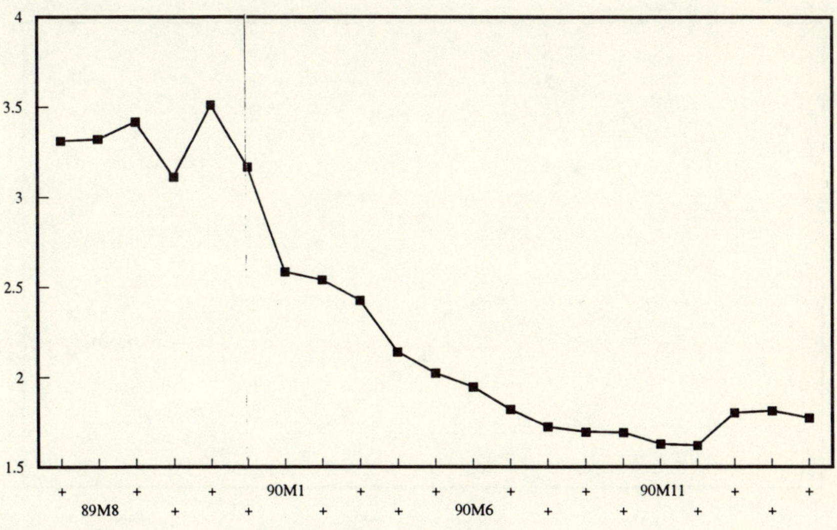


**Figure 4.6** Yugoslavia 1989–91: reserve money to narrow money

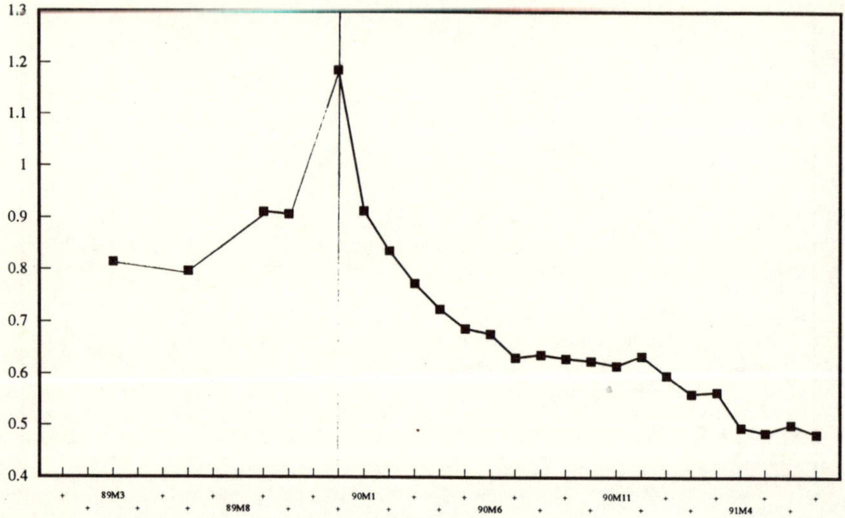


**Figure 4.7** Poland 1989–91: reserve money to broad money

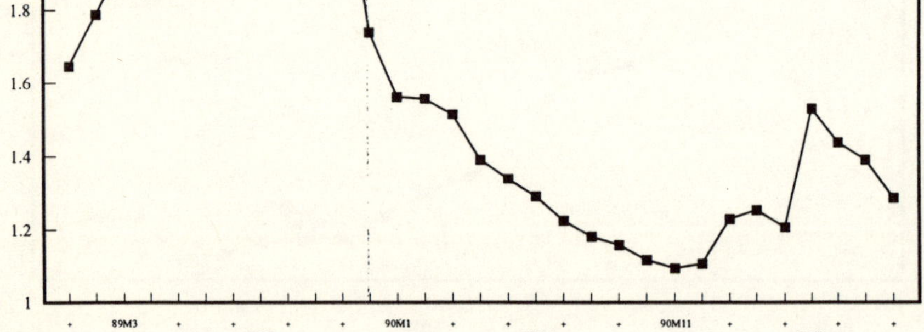


**Figure 4.8** Yugoslavia 1989–91: reserve money to broad money

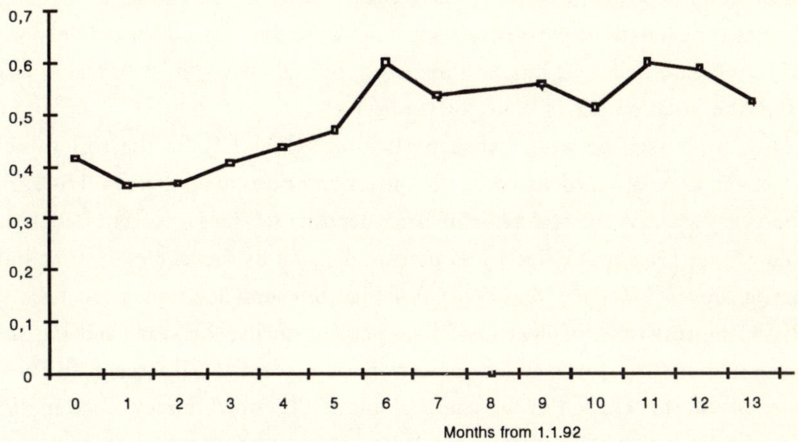


**Figure 4.9** Russia 1992–3: reserve money to narrow money

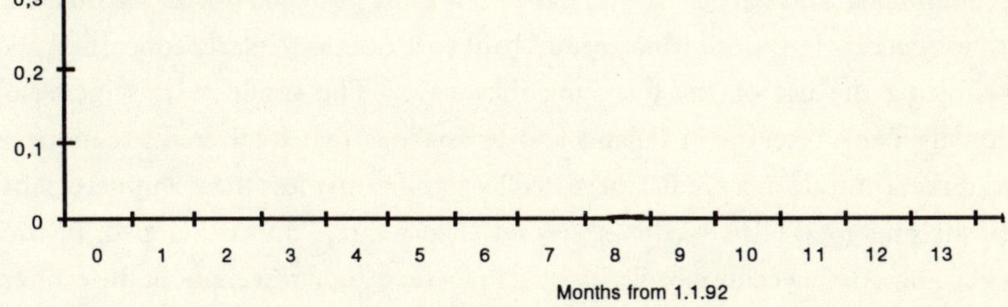


**Figure 4.10** Russia 1992–3: reserve money to broad money

paradoxically in cash. The shift into cash can occur when payment delays through the banking system are such that the effective inflation tax on using cash is lower than on bank deposits (because of the lower velocity of circulation of the latter). Of course, the length of payment delays is not a purely exogenous variable – banks tend to increase delays as inflation increases, as this allows them to take a larger part of the inflation tax revenue for themselves.

Thus in Russia, between February 1992 and March 1993 the real value of currency in circulation (deflated by the consumer price index) increased by almost 20 percent, whereas the real value of bank deposits fell by 17 percent deflated by the consumer price index, and by 44 percent deflated by the wholesale price index (*Russian Economic Trends*, May 1993). A similar phenomenon took place in Poland in 1989: the real value of deposits fell 66 percent during the year,[3] and the share of cash in zloty broad money increased from 28 percent to 37 percent. In Russia, as a result of this change in the composition of the broad money stock in 1992, the structure of financing of total credit (to government, non-government and to the other CIS states[4]) has shifted sharply away from bank deposits and towards CBR credit. In February 1992 this structure was 75:25 (bank deposits: CBR credit), and by March 1993 it was 46:54.[5] Thus, as households and firms are driven out of bank deposits by high inflation and massively negative real interest rates, the CBR is sucked ever more deeply into becoming the lender of first resort to the government, Russian enterprises and foreign (CIS) governments, as well as the dominant source of financing for the banking system. Again a similar phenomenon occurred in Poland, with central bank credit accounting for 60 percent of bank financing in December 1989.

The increased financing of commercial banks by the central bank was accompanied in both Poland and Russia by a sharp increase in voluntary reserves held by commercial banks at the central bank. The most probable reason for this is that with easy access to central bank credit,[6] banks are not particularly concerned about maximizing the use of the financing they have.[7] The result of this increase in voluntary bank reserves in Poland and Russia was that total credit (commercial plus direct central bank credit) increased by significantly less than commercial bank deposits plus total CBR credit. A second vicious circle thus developed, in which the accommodating central bank, wishing to increase total real credit in the economy, found that a larger and larger proportion of the credit it creates ends up "uselessly" deposited back with itself.

Upon stabilization the shrinking of the money multiplier is reversed. The reduction in the degree to which real interests rates are negative[8] causes an increase in households' and firms' desire to hold bank deposits and thus an increase in the money multiplier. Thus in Poland after stabilization, between January 1990 and July 1991, the zloty money supply increased *sevenfold* without any increase in central bank credit during these nineteen months.[9] There were two reasons for this: First, thanks to the real undervaluation of the zloty at the new fixed exchange rate, a large amount of base money was coming into the economy through the non-interest current account surplus, so that there was less call for base money creation by the central bank. Second, the increase in the money multiplier allowed a given amount of base money to support a growing amount of deposit money after stabilization.

## 3 The dilemmas of post-stabilization monetary policy

Thus, during the stabilization of a high inflation the money supply is a "doubly geared" instrument, which makes it difficult to use with any kind of precision. The first "gear" is the well known effect by which stabilization leads to an increase in the demand for money (reduction in the velocity of circulation), so that a given increase in the money supply will have a smaller effect on the price level given a lower expected rate of inflation (e.g. Dornbusch and Simonsen, 1987). Of course, the expected rate of inflation is not entirely independent of increases in the money supply, which makes for interesting dilemmas for policy makers! The second "gear" is the increase in the money multiplier after stabilization, which results in an increase in the money supply which can be far greater than the increase in base money. This second gear is, of course, a result of the first, since it reflects an increase in the demand for domestic deposit money relative to domestic cash and/or foreign currency (cash and deposits).[10]

Clearly, the two gears work in "opposite directions", the one increasing the demand for money, while the other increases its supply. Is there a "Say's law" in reverse, in operation in the monetary sphere during the stabilization of high inflation, with increases in the demand for money creating its own supply? Does this mean that policy makers can count on the effects of these two gears cancelling each other out? To the extent that this is the case, it follows from the institutional fact that during periods of high inflation, most bank deposits are interest bearing. The inflation tax rate is then given not by the rate of inflation, but rather by the rate of inflation less the nominal interest rate.[11] When the degree to which real deposit interest rates are negative is reduced sharply (or eliminated), then both the demand for (interest bearing) money and its supply increases as non-bank actors shift out of cash (and foreign currency[12]) and banks shift out of reserve money, until the maximum size of the money multiplier has been reached. However, the question arises: since in such a case the supply of money is largely endogenous, even when the exchange rate is floating, what then determines the rate of inflation?

A number of monetary policy regimes are in practice possible. The first is to combine the traditional "fine tuning" approach to the determination of the money supply with a flexible exchange rate regime. Guesses are made regarding the amount by which the demand for money is likely to increase, and of the level of the money multiplier in the next period, and base money is adjusted accordingly.[13] Attempts to limit increases in the multiplier may be made by fixing quantitative credit limits for individual banks.[14] Because of the gearing which results from the negative relationship between expected inflation and the demand for real money balances, overshooting is likely in both directions (i.e. policy is likely to be excessively tight when it needs to be tightened and excessively loose when it needs to be loosened). Overshooting is certain if the "gearing" is not taken into account, as in the proposed Ukrainian monetary policy rule for 1993 (Savchenko 1993), which intended to limit money supply growth to 80–90 percent of expected inflation in the next period. Even if the rule simply sets a decelerating rate of growth of the money supply, errors in the predicted inflation path will be cumulative, probably causing severe problems with the real values of planned nominal variables such as budget expenditures or the budget deficit/surplus.[15]

The second regime is based on a fixed exchange rate. With a convertible currency this means that the money supply becomes endogenous. However, if convertibility is limited to current account operations plus internal capital account ones (so-called "internal convertibility"), then this is only true in the medium term. Although the money supply has to end up at the level at which prices of domestically produced tradeables are the same as world prices, this will not happen instantaneously with internal convertibility, because it takes time for the requisite amount of money to enter or leave the country through the current account.[16] In the short term monetary policy still matters. If a country begins with an undervalued exchange rate, and domestic money creation is too rapid, then there is a serious danger that the equilibrium price level will be overshot, because today's money supply may determine next month's prices and the current account several months later.[17] Once the current account shifts from surplus to deficit then it becomes likely that the currency will be devalued, creating room for further domestic money creation and the possibility of further overshooting. This was the experience of Poland during 1990–1, mainly because of the policy of the National Bank of Poland, which aimed at a continuous increase in the real money stock.

If the exchange rate can be sustained, the money supply will fall as a result of a loss of reserves, as long as further domestic money creation ceases. The result will then be full stabilization (at a rate of inflation at which the country's international reserves are stable). However, reserves may be insufficient to sustain the exchange rate. More probably, the loss of competitiveness and the increase in unemployment resulting from the maintenance of an overvalued exchange rate may result in irresistible political and economic pressure (the latter in the form of capital flight) for a devaluation. Once this has happened, monetary policy will once again become important as a means of ensuring that overvaluation does not recur.

For countries in Russia's situation there seem to be two possible styles of monetary policy: the "controlling" and the "laisser aller", the former can be best applied to a fixed exchange rate regime while the latter can be applied to either regime. The "controlling" approach attempts to ensure that the broad money supply evolves in line with international reserves, so that as domestic prices of tradeables rise towards world prices, reducing the rate of increase of international reserves, the rate of increase of broad money declines proportionately. Thus the central bank behaves like a pseudo-currency board of the marginal-fractional kind, with each increase in international reserves by one ruble leading to an increase of a given number of rubles in the money supply (Rostowski, 1993b). The advantage of such an approach is that it allows the economy itself to decide how much nominal money it wishes to hold, since it can always obtain more by running a balance of payments surplus.

The problem, as we have seen, lies in ensuring that the money supply actually increases by the amount desired, since the central bank controls base money but not the money multiplier. As we have noted, quantitative credit limits will help the authorities to control broad money, although at significant microeconomic cost. A better solution would be high reserve requirements (possibly only at the margin) for commercial banks and a high ratio of increases in international reserves to increases in the domestic money supply. The first sets a low upper limit to the money multiplier[18] and also reduces the extent to which deposits are backed by credits, which will reduce the post-stabilization bad debt problem (see Section 5).

If it is impossible to raise reserve requirements on existing deposits, the growth of the money multiplier can be effectively limited by high reserve requirements on increases in deposits.[19] A high incremental international reserves/broad money ratio ensures that if broad money increases much more than intended by the authorities, and the result is that prices of domestically produced tradeables exceed world levels, then at least the international reserves are available to defend the exchange rate.

The alternative style of monetary management available during stabilization is what I call "laisser aller": it can be applied under both fixed and flexible exchange rates, and it may be that Russian circumstances (and national characteristics) might predispose one to this style. It consists in taking advantage of the fact that both the demand for and the supply of broad money will increase as inflation falls, the latter even when the supply of base money remains constant. Combined with a flexible exchange rate regime, the "laisser aller" approach would simply be a matter of terminating the creation of CBR credit overnight. A number of things would then happen more or less simultaneously: 1) real interest rates (both loan and deposit) would increase; 2) both the demand for and supply of money would increase; 3) inflation would fall; and 4) the exchange rate would appreciate.

The question is whether the maximum increase in the supply of money would be sufficient to satisfy the increased demand for money. Clearly, the larger the difference between the pre-stabilization size and the maximum size of the money multiplier, the less the danger of this happening. On the other hand, the greater this difference, the greater the danger of a "bubble" developing, in which the demand for and supply of money increase to such a degree that inflation re-ignites temporarily, and/or the stability of the banking system becomes threatened through an asset price boom-bust cycle.[20]

If there is doubt as to whether the difference between the pre-stabilization and maximum money multiplier is large enough, an additional element of flexibility can be introduced by adopting a fixed exchange rate regime. This allows the economy to increase the stock of base money. The first problem is that if it turns out that there is in fact considerable room for the money multiplier to increase, then the money supply may grow to such an extent that it undermines the fixed exchange rate.[21] The second problem is that one has to choose what level at which to fix the exchange rate.

## 4 Choosing the exchange rate

Excessive undervaluation of the currency is deflationary, because the costs of imported inputs increase rapidly causing a negative supply shock, while the domestic money supply can only expand relatively slowly in accommodation, particularly if tight rules of the kind recommended above are in force. In order to avoid this and the post-stabilization inflation (which is greater the greater the initial undervaluation of the currency), "stabilization funds" have been made a standard part of stabilization programs in PCEs.

The difficulties involved were clearly demonstrated in the Polish stabilization of 1990. The options for the exchange rate which were considered ranged from zl. 9,000:$1, proposed by the National Bank of Poland (NBP) to zl. 14,000:$1 proposed by the Ministry of Foreign Economic Relations (a representative of the exporters' lobby). The IMF proposed a rate of zl. 10,000:$1 and the final compromise was zl. 9,500:$1. The degree of uncertainty was so great that the government would commit itself to this rate only for three months. As it turned out the rate was held for 16 months. Had it not been for the Soviet trade shock of 1991 it could have been held for many months more, even given the NBP's excessively expansionary monetary policy. In these 16 months prices rose 4.6 times. An exchange rate of one-third of that chosen, say zl. 3,500:$1, should therefore have been sustainable in principle in 1990, which would have allowed Poland to avoid the devaluation-driven supply shock it underwent. Thus a common view has been that, given the degree of uncertainty, the currency may not have been undervalued ex ante, but it was definitely undervalued ex post.

It seems, however, that it is far from certain that the rate was undervalued, even ex post, if we mean by this that there existed a far lower rate which would have been in fact sustainable given the expectations at the time. The example of the failed Romanian stabilization of November 1991 is instructive here. The chosen exchange rate of lei 180:$1 gave an average monthly wage of $60. This meant that the lei was less undervalued than the zloty at the beginning of 1990, which gave an average monthly wage of $75 in the first quarter of that year. Nevertheless, with the Polish average monthly wage now at some $220, it seems reasonable to suppose that the Romanian "equilibrium" dollar wage should not be less than $100 per month, so that the Romanian exchange rate of November 1991 still had a very significant cushion of undervaluation built in. Yet, the Romanian authorities lost all of their reserves within a few days of fixing the rate with disastrous consequences.

First, they confiscated all the hard currency accounts of firms, then when this was not enough to save the rate, they abandoned convertibility.[22]

## 5 Bad debts in the banking sector

As we have seen, stabilization leads to an increase in deposit money relative to currency and to an increase in bank credit relative to commercial bank reserves. Thus the importance of central bank liabilities declines, while those of commercial banks increase. Money becomes less backed by the central bank and more backed by the credits which commercial banks have issued. In PCEs this is a particularly acute problem because commercial banks have practically no experience in allocating credit on a commercial basis.[23] Furthermore, real loan interest rates are often high in absolute terms in the immediate post-stabilization period, resulting in borrowers who might have been creditworthy under stable non-inflationary conditions becoming unable to service their debts. This happens just at the time when increasing deposits provide the banks with finance, so that the temptation will be strong to give "evergreen" loans to dubious borrowers by rolling over interest payments due.

In this way a significant stock of bad debt can be built up by the banking sector quite rapidly. In Poland total credit to non-government was the equivalent of about 8 percent of GDP in January 1990. By December of that year it was about 17 percent, a level it has roughly maintained since that time. International audits in mid-1991 showed that about one-third of this credit was classified. Firm level data analysed by Gomulka (1993) suggests that the proportion of problem loans may be closer to 50 percent. If the true value of these loans is half their nominal value, then the additional debt which would accrue to government if it recapitalized the banks would amount to 3-4 percent of GDP.[24] While this is not a very large sum, if handled badly it could lead to severe moral hazard problems in the banking sector, with the government printing money for repeated bank recapitalizations.[25] In Russia the bank credit to GDP ratio is about 14 percent, quite similar to the Polish level before stabilization,[26] so that one could expect any bad debt problem to be of a similar, limited, magnitude. A country such as the Czech Republic, where bank credit is about 80 percent of GDP is potentially in a far worse situation.

The best way of minimizing the bad bank debt problem is to oblige banks to maintain high obligatory reserves and capital adequacy ratios (Rostowski, 1993b).

The former limits the degree to which deposits are backed by bank loans in favour of a greater share being backed by central bank liabilities. The latter ensures that there is a cushion to absorb loan losses before either depositors or the taxpayer have to suffer.[27] Since capital adequacy ratios require that the quality of the portfolio be regularly examined so that necessary provisions be made, and since such skills are largely unavailable in Russia at present, it seems that high reserve requirements can more easily play a useful role under Russian conditions. This requirement for high reserve ratios, and therefore the maintenance of a low money multiplier, suggests that the "controlled" rather than "laisser aller" approach to monetary policy should be preferred. Since it is so hard to determine what the right rate of money growth is during a stabilization, the further implication is that this requirement should be accompanied by a fixed exchange rate regime, to provide a safety valve if the monetary authorities are excessively restrictive.

High reserve ratios mean that for a given level of the money supply there is a lower level of bank credit than otherwise. However, in a PCE in the early stages of transition this is probably an advantage. As Gomulka (1993) has shown, in Poland 60 percent of credit ended up with the 12 percent of firms which have the worst "sales adjusted quick ratios".[28] Moreover, the extremely dynamic private sector has had very little access to credit,[29] financing its very rapid expansion through retained earnings (Rostowski, 1993c). Thus credit in Poland has gone to those to whom it should not have gone (mainly the state sector losers), and has not gone to the winners, in particular not to the rapidly growing private sector, for whom its lack has – interestingly – not proved an insurmountable obstacle. Indeed, one can maybe formulate a hypothesis about the microeconomic *unimportance* of credit in the early stages of transition in a PCE. The explanation for this is probably that liberalization opens up so many new, highly profitable opportunities that the private sector can finance its own rapid expansion with ploughback.[30]

## 6 Inter-enterprise debt: a non-problem?

Recently the magnitude of inter-enterprise debt has diminished sharply in Russia. Whereas payments arrears on the "kartoteka dva" accounted for three trillion rubles (about 50 percent of annual GDP in June 1992.[31] By December the estimate for "accounts receivable" was five trillion rubles, or only about 16 percent of GDP.[32] The question is whether the problem will return in its acute form after stabilization.

The Polish experience (see Rostowski, 1993a) shows that if a stabilization program is credible, inter-enterprise debt (IED) will decline in real terms rather than increasing.

Just how likely this seems in the Russian case depends largely on how one explains the fall in real IED since the summer of 1992. The optimistic explanation for this fall is that the multilateral clearing of IED in August–September 1992 came too late to save the enterprises which had extended this credit from severe loss due to the fall in its real value. In this case, one can be quite optimistic as to the likely behaviour of IED upon stabilization. The pessimistic interpretation would put most of the stress on the very rapid rate of growth of nominal credit since the multilateral clearing exercise. The fact that the ratio of bank credit to non-government/GDP rose only slightly from 12 percent in June 1992 (which was when real IED reached its peak) to 14 percent in March 1993 points towards the optimistic interpretation.

Nevertheless, given the quality of the current data it is as well to be prepared for a surge in IED post-stabilization as in 1992 post-liberalization. The worst thing to do regarding IED is to inject money into the economy. The second worst thing is to perform a multilateral clearing, since this is in effect a government-sponsored equalization of the value of all debtors' inter-enterprise liabilities, and moreover the setting of their real value equal to their nominal value. As such it causes severe moral hazard problems. The best thing to do about a surge in IED is nothing: Latvia, which had an IED/GDP ratio very similar to that of Russia in May 1992, refused to carry out a multilateral clearing, and now has inflation of a few percent per month and a fully convertible currency which has been appreciating against the US dollar.

However, if there are doubts about whether the authorities have the political ability to resist calls for inflationary solutions such as multilateral clearing or money creation, then making IED tradeable should be considered. One of the main reasons for the difficulties surrounding IED is that a properly functioning bankruptcy system does not exist in most PCEs,[33] so that inter-enterprise claims cannot effectively be enforced directly against debtors. If IED is made tradeable then creditors can obtain liquidity by "by-passing" their debtors and selling their claims at a discount to the debtor's debtor. The creditor's liquidity gain is the debtor's loss, as he will not then obtain the money he is owed by his own debtor. For this to work, the debtor's debtor must be able to set the face value of his creditor's liability against his own liability to his creditor, and only be required to pay any residual.

Debtors will, of course, be able to bid for their own liabilities by offering to buy them at a discount in exchange for immediate payment. Tradeable debt is after all the solution which has been generated by the market in the other area in which bankruptcy is impossible – sovereign debt.

The simplest way of ensuring that IED is tradeable is to require suppliers to obtain a proper bill of lading, with the signatures of the relevant authorized persons representing the customer on it. If such a bill is not obtained when goods are delivered, then the goods are deemed by law to be a gift from the supplier to his client. If the bill is obtained it is deemed a formal liability of the client, obliging him to pay within a certain period, and can as such be sold by the supplier at will.

The most important result of such a procedure is that it eliminates the danger of a "liquidity log-jam", by which whole strings of enterprises can claim that they cannot pay each other or (possibly more dangerously) the budget, because they have not themselves been paid. If IED is tradeable it will allow liquidity to flow to where it is most demanded, possibly cutting out whole swathes of non-payers, and at the same time revealing the true revenues of suppliers.[34] In this way, most of the arguments for inflationary solutions to the IED problem will be eliminated. The pressure to increase the money supply, so that it can effect the existing nominal mass of payments due, should disappear when the nominal value of these payments adjusts itself automatically to the existing money supply.

Furthermore, IED trading will, if public, generate useful information regarding the standing of various enterprises. A firm, it suppliers and its direct customers are likely to be as well informed about its financial situation as any group of actors in the economy, and in public auctions of IED, their collective assessment would become available to all. If such auctions existed and one made IED convertible into equity this could be a powerful tool for the privatization of the economy. Something similar is happening in Poland under the "Enterprise and Bank Financial Restructuring Program" (EBFRP): as part of a "compact" between creditors, a bad debtor bank an inter-enterprise debt can be traded and any holder of more than 30 percent of a bad debtor's liabilities can have them converted into equity at par.[35]

## Appendix

In recent stabilizations of high inflation there have been four cases when the ratio of reserve money to broad money increased after stabilization, rather than decreasing (Argentina 1985, Brazil 1986, Israel 1985 and Peru 1990). In the first two cases (Argentina 1985 and Brazil 1986) this accompanied a typical decrease in the ratio of reserve money to narrow money. In the other two cases (Israel and Peru) both broad and narrow money multipliers decreased after stabilization. This "atypical" behaviour is easily explained as regards the first two cases:

$$BM = TD + SD + C \qquad (1)$$

BM = Broad Money, TD = Time Deposits, SD = Sight Deposits and C = Cash. As a result of stabilization there may be a shift from time deposits to sight deposits, as real interest rates may have been more negative on the latter (i.e. sight deposits were more "cash-like"). Now if sight deposits also have higher required reserve ratios then the ratio of total reserve money (which includes reserves held against both types of account) to broad money can increase. At the same time the ratio of total reserve money to narrow money (SD + C) falls as expected. It is simplest to imagine that reserve money is held constant while broad money decreases exclusively as a result of the shift of deposits from time to sight.

A simultaneous fall in the broad and narrow money multipliers upon stabilization (as in Israel and Peru) can occur if the shift into narrow money (be it out of time deposits or foreign currency deposits) is much more into cash than into sight deposits.[36] Since cash is part of reserve money the ratio of reserve money to narrow money (SD + C) can increase. The broad money multiplier also falls because of the reduction in time deposits relative to sight deposits. If a fixed exchange rate regime is in operation, as was the case in Israel in 1985, then both broad and narrow money can increase even though both the broad and narrow money multipliers are decreasing, because reserve money can increase.

## Notes

1. The datum for 1 September 1992 is excluded from the graph. The figure was .765, and seems to have been due to the injection of reserve money which took place to complete the multilateral clearing of inter-enterprise debt (Rostowski 1993a).
2. This is the explanation for the failure of the M2 money multiplier to follow the "typical pattern" in a number of countries (see Section 3).

3. When deflated by the consumer price index. The figure using producer prices was almost the same.
4. Which is effectively to Russian exporters.
5. The actual figures are (in R bn):

| | deposits | CBR credit |
|---|---|---|
| February 1992 | 964 | 325 |
| March 1993 | 8331 | 9646 |

Unlike other central banks, the CBR engages in a significant amount of direct lending to firms. However, this does not affect what is happening in the monetary system: the ever greater role of the CBR in financing credit.
6. Directly in the case of the former *Spetsbanki* in Russia and the state banks in Poland, and via the interbank market in the case of less favoured banks.
7. A second possible reason is that payments delays result in a larger amount of money being held at the central bank, either because there are delays in paying money out by the bank concerned, or because of the need to have a cushion against unexpectedly large payments needing to be made. In both cases payments delays would no longer be the result of a deliberate policy by the banks. The observation that they increase with inflation could then result from either: (1) inflation leading to general economic disorganization leading to payments delays; (2) in PCEs inflation has accompanied liberalization, and liberalization has led to a massive increase in the number of bank account holders in a very brief period, which has in turn led to a sharp increase in payment delays. (I am grateful to Miroslav Kerous for this insight.)
8. They may become sharply positive, particularly in terms of foreign currency if the exchange rate is fixed, as was the case in Poland in 1990.
9. National Bank of Poland Monthly Bulletin, various issues.
10. We have already mentioned how the demand for cash may be relatively higher during a high inflation (as compared to the demand for deposits) because, as a result of payments delays when the banking system is used, the inflation tax can in fact be higher on bank deposits, even though they attract some nominal rate of interest.
11. It is then the repression of deposit interest rates which reduces the demand for real interest bearing money balances, and not just inflation itself. This repression can occur in one of two ways: directly by administrative control, which then calls forth the need for massive central bank credit creation to "fill the financing gap" left by the disappearing deposits, or indirectly via massive central bank credit creation which depresses the nominal interest rate far below the rate of inflation, causing a flight from deposits. Real interest rates are not bid up to positive levels by borrowers because the demand for credit does not respond positively to the same degree to highly negative real interest rates as the demand for interest-bearing money responds negatively. This results from high nominal rates requiring very rapid repayment of the real value of loans, and there always is the danger that refinancing one's real debt may prove difficult.
12. If the exchange rate is fixed.
13. Fortunately in the relatively unsophisticated financial systems of PCEs it is still possible to control base money directly. In more sophisticated systems, the interest rate at which base money is provided is usually the direct control variable. This adds a further "gear" to the relationship between the central bank's control variable and prices.
14. In Poland this led to periods of excess bank liquidity in 1990 and 1991, and combined with interest rate ceilings on loans, it also led to corruption of banks' credit officers.

15. If the predicted monthly inflation path is 100, 90, 80, 70 percent, etc., and a 10 percentage point fall in the monthly inflation rate leads to a 10 percentage point increase in the demand for nominal money balances whereas the authorities expect an increase of only 5 percentage points, then in period 2 the money supply is increased by 95 percent, but inflation in fact goes down to almost 80 percent (the 85 percent percent inflation rate which would result from the authorities error requires a further increase in the demand for nominal money of 2.5 percent, which requires a further 2.5 percent fall in inflation).
16. Unless there is a very large amount indeed of domestic foreign currency holdings. However, Poland, which had foreign currency deposits equal to twice the zloty broad money supply at the beginning of the stabilization, took about a year to achieve this equilibrium state, largely thanks to the negative Soviet trade shock.
17. Unless the exchange is already believed to be overvalued, in which case the effect on the balance of payments may precede that on prices.
18. The multiplier is (1+d)/(r+d), where d is the currency/deposit ratio and r is the reserve ratio. with a 33 percent reserve requirement and a 25 percent cash/deposit ratio, the upper limit to the multiplier is 2.
19. Such high marginal reserve requirements have often been used in Latin America for this very purpose, and were used in the UK in the 1970s (the so-called "corset"). The present author proposed a "corset" on bank assets in Poland in 1990.
20. Such inflation could not persist as long as no additional base money was emitted. The threat to the stability of the banking system is thus the greater danger.
21. The "Currency School" were right that over-issue is possible under just such circumstances (and the "Banking School" were wrong to deny the possiblity).
22. One of the few consolations is that Romania had very few reserves to lose. It is possible that with very low reserves any fixed exchange rate is indefensible, however low it may be in real terms. If this was the case, then in the Polish context the question becomes: given that Poland did have substantial reserves, how much higher could it have fixed the value of its currency? This is a question to which there will now never be an answer, since it requires the repetition of a non-repeatable event.
23. It is very hard to achieve, being unable to repay credits obtained under conditions of massively negative real interest rates such as obtained before stabilization.
24. The actual amount by which the Polish government intends to recapitalize the banks is about $1 billion, or 1 percent of GDP. But this may prove quite inadequate.
25. By delaying its response to the problem and being careful to ensure the "incentive compatibility" of its techniques of recapitalization, it appears that Poland may avoid this problem.
26. I am grateful for the Russian data to Brigitte Granville. In March 1993 commercial bank credit to non-government amounted to 8.7 trillion rubles while monthly GDP was 5.2 trillion rubles. In Poland in December 1989 the ratio of credit to non-government/monthly GDP was about 12 percent.
27. Of course, if bank capital belongs to the state or to SOEs the owners may not be able to exercise effective supervision over managers to encourage the avoidance of loss. This is why bank privatization is so important.
28. QR = (Cash + Receivables - Bank loans - Payments due)/three months sales. Interestingly, these are not the socialist giants one would expect to find in this category. They account for 8 percent of sales, and are thus smaller than average.

29. Some 15 percent of bank credit goes to private firms in Poland, even though the private sector accounts for about 50 percent of GDP and for 70 percent of employment outside the budget sector (60 percent of all employment).
30. But see the contrary view put forcefully by Calvo and Coricelli (1992).
31. At June 1992 prices.
32. I am grateful to B. Granville for the figures for monthly GDP in June and December 1992, which allowed the calculation of annual GDP in June 1992 and December 1992 prices through the simple expedient of multiplying by 12. *Russian Economic Trends* Vol. 1, No. 3 for the June 1992 figure for inter-enterprise debt. The December 1992 figure for receivables was provided by the Russian Government's Centre for Economic Reforms.
33. The existence of a bankruptcy law is not the same as the existence of a bankruptcy system. Only Hungary has an efficient bankruptcy system. Poland has had a law since the beginning of its reforms and a system which is still very inefficient, but is slowly improving. The Czech Republic's bankruptcy law only came into force in April 1993!
34. It is, of course, these and not the formal sales price which must be taken into account in calculating profit and sales taxes.
35. Subject to the approval of the Ministry of Privatization.
36. The reason for the shift out of these kinds of deposits is that with stabilization the inflation tax declines.

## References

Calvo, G. and Coricelli, F. (1992) "Stabilizing a Previously Centrally Planned Economy: Poland 1990". *Economic Policy*, No.14, April, pp. 176-226.

Dornbusch, R. and Simonsen, M. (1988) "Inflation Stabilization: The Role of Incomes Policy and of Monetization", in Dornbusch, R. *Exchange Rates and Inflation*, Cambridge, MA, The MIT Press.

Gomulka, S. (1993) "The Skewed Distribution of Enterprise Assets in Poland". Seminar presented at The London School of Economics, London, March 1992.

Rostowski, J. (1993a) "The Inter-enterprise Debt Explosion in the Former Soviet Union: Causes, Consequences, Cures". *Economic Transformation and Communist Economies*, Vol. 5, No. 2, pp. 131-156.

Rostowski, J. (1993b) "Creating Stable Monetary Systems in Post-communist Economies". *Europe-Asia Studies*, Vol. 45, No. 3, pp. 445–461.

Rostowski, J. (1993c) "The Implications of Rapid Private Sector Growth in Poland". Centre for Economic Performance, Discussion Paper No. 159, July 1993, London.

*Russian Economic Trends*, Quarterly journal of the Centre for Economic Reform, Government of the Russian Federation and Centre for Economic Performance, London School of Economics, Whurr Publishers, London.

Savchenko, O. (1993) "Extracts Highlighting Key Features of the Economic Reform Program". *mimeo*, Kiev.

# 5 Problems in Foreign Trade Regulation in the Russian Economic Reform

*Petr Aven*

The historic role of Yegor Gaidar's Government (at least as it was seen by its members) was to provide an "institutional shock" to the economy, i.e., to destroy the traditional stereotypes and mindset of the centrally-planned economy (CPE). The deepest beliefs had to be changed; the systemic features of the CPE that had been untouchable earlier, were now to be demolished. These features were the absolute dominance of state ownership, the non-convertibility of the currency, huge military spending, and the regulation of almost all prices. The short-term goal was to prove that "the unfeasible is feasible" and to create the basis for a market economy. Although macroeconomic stabilization was proclaimed as the central objective of the Government, by April 1992 it became clear that Gaidar would have to sacrifice this goal for the sake of "marketization" (including privatization and general liberalization). Reform measures that are normal for an established market economy, such as the complete abolition of import subsidies or tax reform, had to be left to the next stage of the reform and, probably, to the next Government.

The main problem was that this institutional shock had to take place during an extremely deep economic crisis. Therefore, the Government had to try to avoid collapse and simultaneously attempt a revolutionary reformation of the system.

From the viewpoint of reform, the foreign trade sphere was a very typical example. It was in a very deep crisis and its regulation mechanism was inefficient and obsolete. Two main issues were on the agenda: the introduction of tariffs and currency convertibility. The significance of these issues was huge, just as the other changes implemented by Gaidar's Cabinet, and were previously unknown to the Soviet economy. Their introduction changed the mentality of economic agents and the heart of the system. However, before we examine what has been done, let us look at foreign trade at the end of 1991, when the reform began.

## Foreign trade performance at the end of 1991

During 1984–91, exports from the territory of the former USSR diminished by more than one-third. Three major reasons for such a decline may be singled out. First and foremost, exports declined due to the sharp decrease in oil extraction and accordingly in exports of oil. Oil export revenues fell from $22 bn in 1986 to about $7 bn in 1991. Second, the collapse of COMECON, which was followed by a radical, though rational, shift to mutual hard currency payments, was an additional reason. Finally, the overall economic crisis also played a role.

A further dramatic slide of exports took place in 1991; during that year exports dropped by 24 percent. In addition to these factors, the general decentralization of decision-making revealed that a large share of trade was unprofitable either to one, or even to both, partners. When making decisions about where to sell and where to buy, the state often based its choices on non-economic grounds (or on no grounds at all). Such a policy could not be acceptable for independent economic agents, such as trade firms or enterprises that did not care about political relations among specific countries but were interested exclusively in mutual comparative advantages. Therefore, the dramatic decline in Russia's trade with countries such as Cuba or India was not a disaster but had an economic rationale.

In the Soviet economy, imports of know-how and modern equipment were always used as an important lever of change. They were supposed to promote import substitution, making the USSR more independent and competitive. In the end of the 1980s imports formed the core of the accelerated development of machine-building. A vast inflow of oil dollars from the middle of the 1970s made domestic consumption of consumer goods also highly dependent on imports. Therefore, the maintenance of high imports has been considered a primary task.

Since exports were decreasing, only two means were available for the support of imports: heavy external borrowing, or the accumulation and "proper" use of the hard currency possessions of domestic holders. From 1985 till 1992, the external debt of the country more than doubled, soaring by almost $50 bn. In 1991 alone, it grew by almost $20 bn. Mikhael Gorbachev regarded new credits ("given to him," as he viewed it) as the salvation of the country. However, debt service absorbed more than one-third of total export revenues in 1991.

Nevertheless, external borrowing was not sufficient, and in 1990 Vnesheconombank started spending its clients' money, later claiming internal bankruptcy. The amount of clients' money that was spent totalled $10.6 bn. Although the clients who were hit were exclusively Soviet entities and citizens, foreign firms which exported goods to the USSR were in fact among the main victims because they were not paid. Mounting arrears in payments for deliveries to the Soviet Union, which had been unknown before, constituted the first blow against lenders' confidence in the Soviet state.

However, despite external and involuntary domestic borrowing, Gorbachev's Government was only able to maintain the level of imports until the middle of 1991. Finally the artificially-maintained imports started plummeting; for 1991 they decreased by 44 percent. In our view, this was the main reason for the decline of production in Russia in 1992.

## Regulation mechanism

The basic principle of organizing foreign trade in a centrally-planned economy was through a state monopoly on foreign trade. The USSR not only had a state monopoly, it even had a monopoly by the Ministry of Foreign Trade until 1985. The absolute majority of firms involved in export or import operations were directly subordinated to this Ministry.

A gradual decentralization of decision making was one of the main developments of the Soviet-type "bargaining economy". At first, branch ministries were given the right to participate in foreign trade: during 1986–8 about half of all foreign trade organizations left the Ministry of Foreign Trade to join different ministries, mainly industrial ministries.

Soon afterwards enterprises gained the right to conduct trade themselves. After 1989 any entity could legally get access to trade, but it was necessary to obtain a special certificate as a "participant in foreign economic activities" in order to begin operations, though it was fairly easy to acquire such a certificate.

All export was also regulated by licensing, but again it was fairly easy to receive a license for exporting anything except raw materials and military equipment. Export licenses were issued by the central USSR Government, and the distribution as well as the certification of exporters became a major source of corruption.

When the approaching collapse of the USSR became obvious, republican authorities, along with the all-union bureaucracy, obtained the right to issue licenses. As an immediate result, the scope of licenses for oil and oil products exports almost exceeded the quantities of extracted and refined oil by the end of 1991.

The sharing of export earnings between an exporter and the state was regulated by hundreds of "currency coefficients", i.e. individualized exchange rates (specific not only to goods, but also to enterprises). The system of multiple rates was intended to introduce some order and fairness into the relationship between exporters and the budget, while domestic prices remained regulated. In reality, "currency coefficients" turned into another bargaining point, and the amounts of hard currency that were left at the exporting enterprises' disposal gradually grew larger.

Imports were controlled through the centralized distribution of hard currency. Similar to the distribution of export licenses and revenues, currency for imports was allotted on a bargaining basis. Hard currency constraints remained "soft" for imports of modern technology and consumer goods, and since the official (and unrealistically high) exchange rate (1.6 rubles per dollar at the end of 1991) was applied to all buyers of hard currency, import subsidies grew to 20 percent of GNP. Tariff regulation for both export and import was basically non-existent.

After the collapse of the USSR at the end of 1991, the situation in Russia was aggravated by the absence of state borders and a desperately obsolete banking system.

## Reforms of 1992

### *Administrative (non-tariff) regulation*

The substitution of administrative foreign trade control by a usual system of tariffs was the first task of the reform in foreign trade. Unnecessary restrictions, such as the certification of foreign trade participants, had to be abolished as well. However, the first step of the Gaidar Government ran contrary to liberalization: all previously-issued licenses for the export of oil and oil products (for a total of $1 bn) were annulled. This step was politically controversial, but it showed the decisiveness of the new Government and its will to play by the rules. The rest of the measures introduced since January 1, 1992 may be regarded as liberal. Thus, the process of certifying foreign trade participants was abolished and all economic entities acquired equal privileges to export and import.

The list of commodities subject to export quotas and licenses was cut considerably. At the beginning of 1992, the list still included oil and oil products, gas and coal, metals, fertilizers and a few other chemical products, timber, fish, and weapons. In the course of the year, this list continued to shrink; ferrous metals, coal and some fertilizers were removed. No civilian machinery required export licenses. Despite that the Government succeeded in significantly reducing the number of goods restricted by export quotas, it was heavily criticized for its lack of radicalism. Critics, and the IMF team in Moscow, considered the preservation of any quotas unnecessary.

Rightly, critics noted that these commodities which remained subject to export quotas stood for more than 70 percent of total Russian exports. Nor is there any doubt that the export tariffs that had been introduced were theoretically sufficient to control the exported volumes of these goods. Nevertheless, it was (and is) necessary to preserve a certain amount of administrative control, for reasons which I shall explain below.

The first of these issues is supplies of key products, such as oil. A sharp decline in the supply of a number of strategic resources to the domestic market is unacceptable. There are purely technical reasons for maintaining the minimal supply of oil to the domestic market, currently amounting to 250–270 mn tons per year. If this amount of oil does not reach Russian enterprises today, losses in industry will be excessive both from a political viewpoint and from the viewpoint of efficient adjustment. Remember that the domestic price of oil was only 3 percent of the world price, and the Russian economy's traditional orientation towards cheap inputs could not be overcome overnight. Even more important, attempts to alter prices overnight might be extremely destructive. To find a road between the inefficient use of resources (from the comparative advantage standpoint) and the collapse of industry was a key task of the Government in 1992. I believe that, in principle, the Government has chosen the right speed: for example, the domestic oil price is now equal to 30 percent of the world price. A better result could hardly have been reached in one year, especially in the difficult Russian political environment.

This issue concerns more than oil; according to government assessments, domestic supplies of various commodities were minimal in 1991-92. The implication is that there was no more room for further increases of certain exports. That is why restrictions on exports is a reasonable choice for the Russian economy, and full liberalization was required only for those export goods needing promoting.

The second issue is domestic pricing. Regulation through export tariffs alone is feasible only if prices are relatively stable. In an environment of permanently and hazardously swinging domestic prices, the task of regulating exports by tariffs alone would require weekly alterations and amendments, which is practically impossible. And after prices were liberalized in Russia, no price stability could be expected.

Moreover, the prices of certain exportable goods (oil, coal, gas) were not liberalized at all in January 1992. Therefore, attempts to regulate significant exports solely by tariffs would have been senseless.

An additional reason for temporarily controlling exports by administrative means is that as long as state ownership prevails, managers care little about economic rationale from the enterprises' point of view, though they do care about personal benefits, such as bribes and foreign travel. In 1991, for example, non-ferrous metals were being sold at only 20 percent of the world price in a few cases. Therefore, purely economic regulation was not sufficient for all situations — price control through licensing was necessary.

Due to the reasons mentioned above, the Government saw its task as the introduction of a system of tariff regulation, but not as the immediate abolition of administrative control over exports. Economic agents had to be used to pay export duties. Only later, when these payments had become common and the system sufficiently advanced, should administrative control get completely eliminated. The Government planned to conclude this work during 1993–4, and the introduction of export tariffs in 1992 was regarded as a first step in that direction. At this first stage export tariffs and quotas (and licenses) had to co-exist.

Let me remind the reader that other economies in transition also used non-tariff control over exports at the beginning of their economic reforms. In Poland in early 1990, export restrictions were introduced for 24 items. In Czechoslovakia in 1991, about 20 percent of merchandise exports remained controlled through licensing.

However, the system of allocation of export quotas had to be revised drastically. Since January 1, 1992, the formalities of licensing were radically altered in order to become more expedient and "automatic".

The Ministry of the Economy was given the task of determining the total quotas for exports of certain goods from Russia. It was to forward these quotas through various branch ministries to export-producers and regional authorities. It was presupposed that the producers' quotas would be allocated in proportion to the production capacity of their facilities. Regional quotas, which were to be supervised by the respective local administration had to be equal to 10 percent of all the quotas given to the local producers. Like other goods, quotas could be bought and sold.

Provided that both export quotas and export contracts were available, the Ministry of Foreign Economic Relations was to issue export licenses. Thus, the role of an export license was purely price control. The Ministry of Foreign Economic Relations was also supposed to receive a part of national export quotas (though rather limited in 1992) for sales through auctioning. The idea of auctioning was to execute state obligations, primarily with regard to politics and foreign debt, and to ensure the flexibility of the internal transformation process.

In general, the intentions of up-dating the administrative supervision was to eliminate discretionary choices and to reduce the leeway of central authorities to determine who would carry out exports. It was a major anti-corruption measure. Imports, however, were not affected by any administrative interventions.

Even in Czechoslovakia, four categories of commodities (crude oil, gas, drugs, arms and munitions) remained subject to import licensing in 1991, and later some agricultural products were added to this list. In Hungary annual quotas were introduced in 1992 on imports of 15 various steel products from Czechoslovakia and the republics of the former USSR. Thus, from this viewpoint, Russia and Poland were more "liberal".

### *Tariff regulation*

Export tariffs, which were introduced in the beginning of 1992, covered almost the same articles that were subject to administrative controls. Tariffs did not apply to those goods that were export priorities, such as machinery and the majority of other industrial goods. Currently, export tariffs vary from 20 to 30 percent of the world market price. As domestic prices approached world market prices, the level of export tariffs was to diminish gradually. This process has in fact taken place in 1992–3.

The introduction of export tariffs came as a shock to a large number of exporters who had been extracting excess profits from their trade. It also came as a shock to certain foreign importers and countries, such as Finland, whose prosperity was heavily based on cheap imports from Russia. By setting the level of tariffs as a percentage of the world price, exporters could not escape the tariffs by understating prices.

As a result, the pressure on the Government to abolish the new tariff system was strong from exporters. Some exporters stopped exports and tried to show that these new tariffs made all trade unprofitable. The drastic decrease of exports in the beginning of 1992 was at least partially artificial: exporters hoped that the new system would be eliminated. To tell the truth, this decline was also brought about by certain technical mistakes and the lack of coordination between the Government and the Central Bank in the installation of the export duties payment system. But the Government was able to withstand the pressure, and while making certain changes in the level of tariffs in February, and some exemptions from payments, it preserved the system. In 1993 tariffs became a stable source of income for the budget.

With due consideration to the extraordinary monopolization of the Russian economy and the collapse of domestic supply, at the end of 1991, the Government decided to refrain from introducing any import tariffs and to remove all obstacles to accelerated imports. The under-valued ruble itself played the role of an import tariff. During the first six months of 1992 import tariffs did not exist.

However, harder budget constraints and growing rivalry among suppliers made the industrial lobby cry out for protectionist policies. Also, purely fiscal considerations brought forth by the IMF resulted in a unified 5 percent import tariff, introduced in July 1992, and rising to 15 percent in September.

The level of tariffs introduced in Russia was similar to those chosen in other economies in transition "from Marx to the market". At the start of liberalization, the average level of import tariffs was 16 percent in Hungary, 12 percent in Poland, and 5 percent in Czechoslovakia, where it later was significantly increased.

The ability to introduce more advanced (non-unified) tariffs in Russia in 1992 was very limited. Nobody could tell which industries actually needed protection that would be efficient from the medium-term viewpoint. However, starting in January 1993, import tariff rates were diversified. Currently the tariff is zero for foodstuffs and pharmaceuticals, 5 percent for raw materials and semi-processed items, and 15 percent for ready-made goods.

Until 1993 imports were not subject to any additional taxation in the form of excises or value-added tax. But in January 1993 these were introduced. The list of goods subject to excise taxes is similar to the corresponding domestic list, though tax rates may vary. Vodka, of which production fell sharply in 1992 in Russia, is the one example of different levels of excises.

### *Currency regulation*

Although currency exchanges were already operating in Russia in 1991, before 1992 the purchasing of hard currency for imports was troublesome, if at all possible. Enterprises had long stayed in the dark about how to purchase hard currency, which was fully in keeping with the spirit of a barter economy. Hard currency, just like everything else, was another "bargaining item", and it was not considered decent to buy it at outrageous prices, but it was acceptable to squeeze it out of the Government. When the Minister of Foreign Economic Relations, speaking in Parliament, announced for the first time that in the following year all importers would have to, and would be able to, buy hard currency from banks, the MPs began to laugh. The common argument was: "There is not enough currency in the country to buy".

As regards the consumer market, for decades it had been alienated from hard currency, whose circulation was strictly forbidden, with the risk of criminal persecution for the disobedient. In this environment, it is quite understandable that the task of completely reforming the currency regulation system was the most important part of reforming the foreign trade mechanism.

As a first step, the multiple "currency coefficients" (exchange rates) were abolished. Exporters were obliged to surrender 40 percent of their hard currency earnings at the fixed rate of 55 rubles per dollar to the Central Bank. At the time 55 rubles was equal to 50 percent of the auction rate. (For private citizens, a different black-market rate did exist, which was slightly higher than the auction rate.) An additional 10 percent of revenues had to be surrendered to banks at the auction (market) exchange rate.

The rate of 55 rubles per dollar arose as a compromise between the Government and the Central Bank, which had insisted (with the silent backing of some officials from the Ministry of Finance) on preserving either multiple surrender coefficients or on introducing a fixed artificial rate, proposed at the unrealistic level of 3 rubles per dollar. Later the proposed figure grew to 5.4 rubles which was regarded to be high enough, taking into consideration the official rate used then for importers: 1.6 rubles per dollar.

The level of the exchange rate was not the main thing, though the level proposed by the Government was tied to the level of export tariffs. What did matter was to break the old way of thinking which viewed hard currency not as "money", but simply as an ordinary commodity, taken (not bought) by the Government from those who possess it, and allocated by the Government, again for free.

Two tasks had to be solved in order to destroy this old pattern of behavior. First, exporters had to be paid for the currency they surrendered to the state, and the price had to be real. It did not matter whether the price was 40 or 60 rubles per dollar, but the non-price of 3–5 rubles had to go. Moreover, this price had to be unified, and the bargaining connected with currency coefficients had to be avoided.

Second, importers also had to be forced to pay the real price for hard currency. And this price naturally had to be equal to the price paid for the currency by the state. In other words, the Central Bank's surrender rate had to be equal to the rate applied for importers who received hard currency from the Government. The rate set at currency auctions was to be used in all transactions except those that were state-related.

Of course, using an artificial exchange rate instead of the auction rate had no economic rationale. However, in January the Government was not powerful enough to push beyond this compromise. After the extremely low rates (both for surrender and purchasing) were abolished, it was much easier to implement a unified market exchange rate later in July.

From July 1992, the exchange rates for hard currency surrender, currency auctions and "purchase-for-import" were actually unified. The auction (market) rate applied to all transactions, with a few exceptions, such as "centralized imports". From that time 20 percent of hard currency earnings were to be sold compulsorily through the currency market, and another 30 percent to the Central Bank. However, the market (auction) exchange rate was employed in both cases, and it is based on the rate set at Moscow Interbank Exchange Auctions which took place once a week in 1991 increased to twice a week in 1992.

In discussing the reform I would like to mention that it was especially difficult to overcome the habit of importers of technological equipment to receive hard currency for free. Their main argument was: "Nobody has enough rubles, you will stop the country." A similar argument ("There are not enough rubles") was used by certain Ministry of Finance officials when the problem of currency surrender was discussed. Obvious answers, such as: "The state will receive rubles from the export duties and from those who buy the currency", or: "If you would like to subsidize, do it directly, but not through the exchange rate" did not always help. In fact, during the whole year the Government used special "subsidy coefficients" applied to imports of certain goods if it took place by a Government decision within centralized imports. These were in fact individualized exchange rates. However, in the second half of the year centralized imports began to evaporate, so the role of these coefficients decreased drastically. At the end of 1992, only a small number of foodstuffs (mainly grain and sugar) were actually subsidized through the exchange rate.

The unification of the exchange rate and the reduction of import subsidies was backed up by a new procedure for distributing hard currency credits received under Government guarantees. Instead of their nearly free allotment (at the official rate of 1.6 rubles per dollar) with vague requirements for re-payment, a compulsory 15 percent pre-payment of the utilized credit was introduced in July. Payment had to be made in rubles based on the market exchange rate. Also, the enterprises had to pay for the received credits in full compliance with their terms. As a result there was a serious decline in the number of enterprises' requests for hard currency credits.

One controversial question that remained on the agenda was obligatory surrender. From my point of view it was justified to push the economic system, even artificially and administratively, towards the creation of an adequate currency market. Regretfully, the overthrow of the finance and banking system brought about a notable time gap between when hard currency was surrendered by an exporter and when the ruble equivalent of sold hard currency ended up in exporter's account. This gap sometimes exceeded two months. Given the heavy inflation, this meant an additional export tax of at least 20 percent. Apart from that, some exporters had a special relationship with their banks, which made it possible to avoid obligatory surrender. However, artificial support to the hard currency market, as in the beginning of 1992, helped to spread know-how of currency operations and promoted a gradual growth in the amount of hard currency offered for sale and purchase.

In fact, the new mechanism of hard currency regulation allowed residents to enjoy current account convertibility. Moreover, import contracts were sometimes faked, which means that hard currency in reality was bought and sold without any real commitment. The private currency market has now been completely legalized. I strongly believe that ruble convertibility was one of the major achievements of the Gaidar Government.

### *Special exporters*

As mentioned earlier, state ownership affects the behavior of enterprise managers, who are frequently more interested in their personal income than in gaining maximizing export revenues for "their" companies. Underinvoicing became an acute problem in 1991–2. The lack of experience and amateur rivalry between many newly-emerged exporters led to falling prices on several major export items. Antidumping procedures aimed at Russian exporters became common in Europe, US and Japan; ferrous metals and fertilizers were frequently under investigation.

The Government realized that it was impossible to control prices exclusively through licensing. There were also political considerations which forced the Cabinet to show that it would not "sell out" Russia. It was decided to decrease the number of exporters in those spheres where underpricing was most common. The idea was to make it possible to monitor exporters of "strategic" commodities. From autumn 1992 permission to export "strategic" goods, such as oil and oil products, gas, ferrous and non-ferrous metals, and timber, was granted only to "skilled exporters".

In practice, the list of "strategic" goods was almost the same as the list of goods subject to export quotas. (The former was even a bit larger.) Through this step all items were clearly divided into two groups. The first group embraced commodities covered by all forms of export control: quotas, licenses, tariffs and certification of exporters. The second group included goods that could be freely exported. Obviously, raw materials constituted the core of the first group, and goods with a relatively high level of processing belonged to the second. Only a few items were in between. Thus, ferrous metals were not subject to export quotas, but had to be traded through "special exporters" and with export tariffs.

I have to admit that the introduction of "special exporters" was a mistake (or an unnecessary concession). In principle, it could have made sense if the number of exporters could truly have been limited, as when this system was initially introduced in September 1992. At that time the list of "special exporters" embraced all major producers of relevant commodities, and also those trade organizations which have proved to be competent. In general, the number of exporters was reduced several times. However, under strong pressure from enterprises, the list of "special exporters" started to grow again, and it grew several times. Similar to the "participants of foreign trade" in 1991, now almost everyone can acquire the necessary permission, and thus it is yet another source of bribes and corruption.

One important lesson can be drawn from this experience, namely, that any obstacle to economic activity, especially one which assumes the existence of a discretionary choice, will be circumvented in Russia, and therefore, this country has to be more liberal than any other.

Certain steps have been taken in 1992 in the area of trade policy and export promotion, but they were not of a very reformist nature.

## Results of 1992

In my view, the foreign trade performance in 1992 was generally satisfactory. For the first time since 1989, the monthly volume of exports stopped falling and even started to grow. The physical volume of exports in 1992 was even with 1991. Due to the slump in world market prices, export revenues fell by 12 percent, to $45 bn. If we do not count the "gratuitous" part of 1991 exports (to countries such as Cuba or Mongolia), the drop could be assessed at a mere 7 percent.

Imports in 1992 decreased by 6 percent, to $42 bn. Imports fell less than exports, due to the lower share in Russia of all-union imports (63 percent) as compared to exports (80 percent). Contrary to the previous year, the trade balance was positive at $3.1 bn. The current account balance was negative at 3.0 bn.

The creation of an adequate hard currency market was another success of the reform. In January 1992 the monthly currency exchange turnover totalled only $18 mn. It came close to the billion mark by the end of 1992, equaling one-third of exports. At least the same amount was sold by banks outside the auctions. The ruble proved to be de facto convertible for current transactions.

When the new Government took office in November 1991, state hard currency reserves were less than $100 mn. By the time Yegor Gaidar resigned, they were more than $1.5 bn. During first five months of 1993 this figure increased at least threefold.

The dynamics of the exchange rate were also positive. Within the first six months of 1992, the dollar became 15 times cheaper in real terms in Russia. From November 1992 until March 1993, the dollar again depreciated twofold against the ruble. While the nominal ruble exchange rate fell by about 15 percent a month, the average monthly inflation rate was 20–25 percent. The appreciation of the ruble (not only in real terms, but later even in nominal terms) continued into 1993. However, foreign trade performance, and in particular exports, responded slowly to the ups and downs of the exchange rate. According to our estimates, only ferrous and nonferrous metals exports correlated modestly with the exchange rate fluctuations.

Due to the introduction of the tariff system, export and import revenues became a stable source of income for the budget. Now they account for about 20 percent of all budgetary revenues. This figure could be much larger if numerous regions and enterprises had not been granted tariff privileges.

Unfortunately, the number of exemptions from export or import duties is not decreasing. In 1992 about 100 decrees of the Government or of the President gave tariff privileges for a total sum of more than $2.8 bn ($2.5 bn for exports, $0.3 bn for imports). During the first three months of 1993 new privileges were given for $3.6 bn.

In principle, the first quarter of 1993 exceeded most of the trends achieved in 1992. However, the introduction of a value-added tax and excises for imports resulted in a notable decrease of imports (by nearly 50 percent), while exports stayed even. As a result, Russia had a positive balance of trade in the first three months of 1993 totaling $5 bn. After four months, the trade surplus reached $7.6 bn.

Although certain attempts to partially centralize trade took place in the beginning of 1993, they did not change the basic features of the system introduced in 1992. Moreover, the majority of decisions made continued at the pace initiated a year before. Thus, certain goods were excluded from the list of goods subject to export quotas (for example, timber).

As before, exporters have to surrender 50 percent of their hard currency earnings, but now only to commercial banks and not to the Central Bank. Therefore, state intervention has become less important and the supply of hard currency on the market more guaranteed.

The subsidization of imports has been decreasing gradually. As early as 1992, import subsidies fell from over 20 percent to 5–6 percent of GNP, and I hardly believe that the Government could have done better at the time. However, centralized imports were further decreased in 1993, and now it appears that only grain will be subject to further import subsidization.

Thus, in concluding, it seems that the reform of the foreign trade sphere has become irreversible.

# 6 Privatization in Russia: An Overview

*Anatoly B. Chubais and Maria D. Vishnevskaya*

Privatization in Russia started in earnest in January 1992. On 1 January 1992, only 70 enterprises were in private ownership by citizens, and 922 enterprises were in collective ownership. By April 1993 the progress of Russian privatization was substantial. A total of 61,810 enterprises had been privatized, or 25.2 percent of all enterprises operating as independent legal entities. According to data of the State Statistics Committee of Russia (Goskomstat), 90 percent of all privatized enterprises had been profitable before privatization. 114,725 applications for privatization had been submitted compared to 1,500 by January 1992, and 61,810 or 54 percent of these had been completed.

In 1992, revenues from privatization for the whole year were only 157 bn rubles. But in 1993, revenues had reached twice this level by May 1, amounting to a total of 370 bn rubles throughout Russia. The deals concluded in the first four months of 1993 total to approximately 200 bn rubles. About 100 bn rubles, or 50 percent of the total revenues to the budget, are in the form of vouchers. Even so, revenues of 100 bn rubles in a four-month period represent a rather substantial sum.

As Table 6.1 shows, the progress of privatization from January to March 1993 is much greater than the same period in 1992.

The development of small-scale privatization has been dynamic. By the beginning of April 1993, the total number of privatized enterprises was 61,810, or 52 percent of the total. Sales prices per unit averaged at 8.99 times the starting prices. The share of private enterprises in trade in mid-1993 thus amounts to 52.3 percent of the total of former state enterprises; in public catering, 47.0 percent; and in consumer services, 52.9 percent.

Turning to the corporatization of large enterprises (those with over 50 mn rubles of fixed assets and over 10 thousand employees) a total of 4,786 enterprises have been included in the list for mandatory corporatization. By the beginning of April

1993, 1,919 privatization plans had been approved and the number of registered joint stock companies reached 1,387.

Even many medium-sized enterprises which were not included in the list for mandatory corporatization have set up working commissions to prepare for corporatization. By May 1993, 9,020 such enterprises had done so. By 1 April 1993, more than 17 thousand large and medium-sized enterprises were in some stage of corporatization, and local privatization committees have already adopted a decision on the transformation of about 9,000 such enterprises into open joint stock companies.

**Table 6.1** Privatization progress throughout Russia (averages)

| | Rates of applications submitted[a] | Rates of applications completed[b] | Actual rates of privatization[c] | Intensity of privatization[d] |
|---|---|---|---|---|
| Averages for 1992 | 0.430 | 0.457 | 0.197 | 0.369 |
| January 1993 | 0.446 | 0.502 | 0.224 | 0.421 |
| February | 0.459 | 0.515 | 0.237 | 0.445 |
| March 1993 | 0.468 | 0.539 | 0.252 | 0.474 |

a. number of applications submitted/number of independent state enterprises
b. number of applications resulting in completed sale/number of applications submitted
c. number of applications resulting in completed sale/number of independent state enterprises
d. number of applications resulting in completed sale/number of enterprises subject to privatization

## Vouchers: fluctuating market value

The progress in corporatizing enterprises can be described as the "supply side" in the mass privatization. The "demand-side" is represented by privatization checks (vouchers) and check (voucher) auctions.

Privatization vouchers were distributed from 1 October 1992 to 31 January 1993 under the supervision of the State Committee for Property Management (Goskomimushchestvo, or GKI). During those four months, about 144 mn people, or 96 percent of the population of Russia, fetched their privatization vouchers, which were distributed by the local branch offices of the Russian Federation's Savings Bank. The nominal value of one voucher is 10,000 rubles, but the market value is subject to considerable fluctuations. Two types of factors have influenced the market price of a voucher.

The first factor relates to regulatory changes. The market price reflects decisions by the Government or the President, and policy resolutions of the GKI, which determine, for instance, what share of property that can be bought for vouchers, and the terms of voucher investments. The second, and most important, factor is the political situation in Russia. Three stages of market value behavior for the voucher can be traced to the political scene.

1 From 1 October until mid-December 1992, the voucher enjoyed a relatively high market price, at between 7,000–10,000 rubles.
2 From January until the beginning of May 1993, the value of the voucher fell sharply, but stabilized again. The period of the formation of the new Government, an internal governmental struggle, and the Supreme Soviet's fierce opposition to the privatization program of the Government corresponded to a fall in the price of a voucher to 3,990 rubles by 2 February 1993 and a gradual stabilization at 4,000–4,200 ensued by the beginning of May.
3 In mid-May 1993, the voucher price grew by 100–150 rubles a day up to 8,300–8,600 rubles on average throughout Russia. In peak periods at certain exchanges it was as high as 12,000 rubles. This appreciation can be traced chiefly to the results of the referendum on 25 April. The increase in the voucher price was also stimulated by a number of powerful decisions by the President of the Russian Federation and the Government, in particular, the Presidential Decree "On the State Guarantees for the Right of Citizens of Russia to Participation in Privatization" and the arrangements made between the GKI and the Russian Ministry of Fuel and Energy for the sale of some property of the fuel and energy industry for 30 mn vouchers.

## Voucher auctions: procedures

Voucher auctions began on the basis of normative documents worked out in the GKI. The local privatization agencies ("property funds") are charged to supervise the organization of auctions, and to sell shares of any enterprise in accordance with their privatization plan. Moreover, the local property funds are to publish official information about the coming biddings at least one month before the last day of an auction.

This information is published in one of the central newspapers, in the case of large enterprises, and in the local press, for small ones, as well as in the Bulletin of the Russian Federal Property Fund. The information should include data about the number of shares to be sold at the auction, the nominal price of one share, the date of the auction, and the financial standing (including balance sheet for the last year) for all the enterprises offering their shares in the auction. After the end of the period for the collection of bids, usually 2–4 weeks, the Commission conducting the auction defines the number of shares one voucher can buy, which is called the "rate" of the auction.

The first 18 voucher auctions took place in December 1992. In January there were 105; in February, 191; in March, 431; in April, 604; in May, 584; and in June, 851 took place. The total amount of property sold through voucher auctions reached 15,150 bn rubles (total statutory capital placed for the voucher auctions) by April 1993. There are no restrictions for participation of foreign physical or legal persons in the voucher auctions.

In the first auctions, an average of about 22 percent of the shares of every enterprise was sold. Later on, the number of shares sold tended to increase, reaching about 29 percent. After the Presidential Decree "On the State Guarantees for the Right of Citizens of Russia to Participation in Privatization" was issued, it became mandatory to sell 29 percent of the shares of privatized enterprises through a voucher auction in the first three months after the registration of a joint stock company.

After January, the average "auction rate" sank steadily. (The auction rate expresses the number of shares, at the nominal value of 1,000 rubles, per voucher.) In January, the rate was above 4; in February it fell to 2.6; in March, 2.55; and in April it reached 1.1. The rapid decline in the rate in April reflects a higher demand (3.5 times compared to March) due to the increasing supply of shares (1.5 times compared to March). At voucher auctions in April alone, the number of vouchers exchanged for shares of enterprises reached 7 mn.

## Regional differences

Some areas are far ahead of others in the organization of voucher auctions, notably St Petersburg (65 auctions), Stavropol (57 auctions), Khakassiya (40) Voronezh, Ivanovo, Vologda, Vladivostok, Kurgan, Kursk, and Mordovia. Territorial and inter-regional auction centres are being opened. The first permanently operating territorial (oblast) auction privatization centre was opened on 8 February, in Volgograd. At the end of February, an inter-regional centre was opened in Moscow, and in May such centres were already operating in many regions. It is expected that setting up auction centres, and at the same time organizing All-Russian auctions to sell shares of the largest enterprises, will greatly facilitate the stabilization of privatization sales. All-Russian and regional auction centres should be opened throughout the country. Together they will form a united national stock market on the basis of the Russian telecommunications stock system, a concept that is currently being elaborated.

## The Russian model of privatization

At present, we have gained sufficient practical knowledge for assessing the Russian mass privatization model in its initial stages, as well as its capacity to be implemented. Our practical experience has vividly confirmed the efficiency of the concept laid out in the State Privatization Program of 1992, which was based on a general and free allotment of property to all citizens of the country, thus maintaining a balance of interests among all participants of the privatization process. And the pace of privatization did not slow down much, even in the face of the tense political struggle over privatization in January–April 1993, at the top level of the Russian administration.

However, many factors have affected the voucher price negatively, such as the resignation of acting Prime Minister Yegor Gaidar at the VII Congress of People's Deputies in December 1991, the debate in the Supreme Soviet of the Russian Federation on the draft of the Law on Privatization Vouchers and amendments to the State Privatization Program of 1993 (called the "fourth alternative" of corporatization, implying a cancellation of vouchers and the transfer of 95 percent of the shares to the work collective), the postponement of the consideration of the Law and the Program in the Supreme Soviet, the announcement that the results of the privatization of public and municipal enterprises in Russia were unsatisfactory, the criticism of the Privatization Program by some members of the Government, and the sharp increase in counter-measures by various industrial ministries and other institutions.

Certain local attempts to halt privatization were also detrimental. The Supreme

Soviet attempted to bring the privatization to a stop "from the bottom", an extremely dangerous move. Chelyabinsk was the first area. On March 18 1993 the regional Soviets decided to "temporarily suspend voucher auctions in the region". Similar decisions were made, or were ready to be made, by the local councils of Novosibirsk, Voronezh, Bryansk, and Barnaul. Opposition to the privatization process has been noted in the regions of Tula, Arkhangelsk, and Lipetsk, as well as in the Northern Caucasus and Bashkortostan.

These attempts were met with resolute measures by the GKI (including a visit by its chairman, Deputy Prime Minister Anatoly Chubais to the Chelyabinsk region, and an appeal to the Procurator-General of Russia, and protests from other regions). These moves succeeded in cancelling the suspension of privatization and thus stopping a probable chain reaction.

## Prospects

Today, in the middle of 1993, we can establish that the great political struggle over privatization in Russia has been completed. The opponents of privatization have sustained a decisive defeat, as confirmed by the referendum of 25 April. This state of affairs allows the leaders of the GKI to turn to a serious analysis of the short and long-term problems of privatization in Russia. Most pressing is the problem of providing support to enterprises after privatization.

In the Russian voucher model of privatization, it is precisely the free distribution of property in society that has considerably strengthened the political support for privatization and for economic reforms, as a whole. However, such a scheme of privatization will not solve several key problems, namely, how to provide an "efficient" owner (at least at the initial stage), effective structural reforms, and capital inflow. Structural re-adjustment will require major investment. The lack of actual capital inflow in 1994 may spell the failure of privatization in Russia, because mass bankruptcy of privatized enterprises could undermine the hard-won confidence in privatization for decades.

That is why the proposal of the US administration to launch a fund for privatization and economic reconstruction in Russia can be a strategic factor in supporting the privatization process. The size of the fund will be $4 bn, and international experience has shown that every dollar invested in intergovernmental business attracts 5–10 dollars of investment in private business.

Creating non-governmental institutions for the support of already privatized enterprises in Russia has a fundamental economic and political importance for the country and for the whole world.

# 7 The Progress of Russian Privatization

*Maxim Boycko, Andrei Shleifer and Robert W. Vishny*

## Introduction

When Anatoly Chubais started to work on Russian privatization in November 1991, the idea of creating private ownership of Russian firms seemed extremely remote. Price liberalization and stabilization were the first priorities of the Gaidar government, and few people seriously discussed privatization as a realistic near-term reform strategy for the Russian economy. Over the next 6 months, Chubais and his team developed a privatization program for Russia[1] that was accepted by the Russian Parliament in June 1992. The implementation of the program started in early 1992 for small firms, and in December 1992 for large firms. Over that period, privatization has become the most significant, lasting, and popular achievement of the Russian reforms.

In this brief paper, we shall describe the progress of large scale privatization in Russia between December 1992 and June 1993. We first briefly describe the outlines of the privatization program, then summarize the results during the period under study. The concluding section discusses the future of Russian privatization.

## The Russian approach to large-scale privatization

As a first step, the Russian program divided firms into those that would be sold for cash by the local governments, and those that would go into the mass privatization program. Essentially, most small shops and some smaller enterprises were immediately allocated to the local governments in this way. Giving them the revenues from small scale privatization was the major concession to the local governments.

As a second step, the program delineated larger firms into five subgroups: those subject to mandatory privatization, those which could privatize on a voluntary basis, those subject to privatization with the permission of the Privatization Ministry (GKI), those requiring government approval for privatization, and those whose privatization was prohibited. Mandatory privatization included firms in the "light" industries, such as textiles, food processing, furniture, etc. Firms requiring GKI approval tended to be somewhat larger firms that did not operate in any of the important strategic industries. Major firms in most strategic industries, such as natural resources, defence, and steel could only be privatized with the agreement of the whole government. Given the anti-reformist composition of the government in 1993, this restriction meant that these firms could generally not be privatized. Even if some part of their equity could be privately owned, control always remained with politicians. Finally, some firms, including those involved in transport, space exploration, health, and education, could not be privatized at all.

As a third step, all large and medium-sized firms except for those in the last list were to be corporatized. That is to say, they were to re-register as joint stock companies with 100 percent of equity owned by the government, a corporate charter, and a board of directors. Initially, the board would have representation by the government, the management, and the workers, as well as supplier and customer managements. Boards of directors did not have any representation by outsiders. The corporatization decree, signed by President Yeltsin in July 1992, was correctly viewed as the first major step toward the subsequent privatization of state firms.

Parallel to corporatization, divisions of state firms had the right to split off and become independent. This proved to be rather difficult because of resistance from the management of the holding company and the local officials. Nonetheless, as we discuss below, such split-offs occurred in many cases.

Once a firm was corporatized, its managers and workers were allowed to choose between three privatization options. The first option gave workers 25 percent of the shares of the enterprise for free, yet made these shares non-voting. Top managers got 5 percent at a nominal price. In addition, after privatization, the workers and the managers could get an additional 10 percent at a low price through something that resembles an ESOP (Employee Share-Owning Program).

The second option gave managers and workers together 51 percent of the equity, all voting, at a nominal price of 1.7 times the July 1992 book value of assets. This of course represented a very low price relative to the market value of these assets in a highly inflationary environment. Workers could pay for these shares in cash, with vouchers (to be discussed later), or through the retained earnings of the enterprise, and could pay over a relatively short period of time. As with the first option, an additional 5 percent of shares could be obtained by managers and workers at low prices through the ESOP.

Finally, a third option, imposed by the managerial lobby in the Parliament, allowed the managers to buy up to 40 percent of the shares at very low prices if they promised not to go bankrupt. For a variety of reasons, this option has hardly been used.

Once the managers and workers selected their benefits option, they could submit a privatization plan that described how the rest of the shares are to be sold. While some enterprises are subject to mandatory privatization, in practice, the filing of privatization plans is almost always voluntary. The principal way in which the sale of shares takes place in Russia is through auctions of shares for vouchers.[2] Every person in Russia was offered a privatization voucher for a small fee, and most people picked them up. The voucher had a denomination of 10,000 rubles; it was supposed to expire at the end of 1993; and it was freely tradable. This voucher was then the sole allowable means of payment in auctions of shares of privatizing enterprises. Each privatizing enterprise carries out its individual voucher auction in the city where it is headquartered, and systems have been developed that enable people to buy shares of firms located in other cities.

The auctions have been designed to make bidding very easy: the principal means of bidding is just to submit your voucher and to get however many shares it buys at the equilibrium price. Because vouchers are tradable, some investors have acquired blocks of vouchers and thus could bid for larger blocks of shares. In a typical company, up to 30 percent of the shares will be sold for vouchers, although the government has been selling smaller stakes in "strategic" enterprises that are privatized.

The fate of the remaining shares remains uncertain. About 5 percent of the number of shares sold in a voucher auction can later be sold for cash by the Property Committees (the local government offices selling the shares), with the proceeds to be used to offset the expenses of privatization, as well as pay bonuses to bureaucrats. This approach has proved highly popular with the Property Committees who want to sell more for cash they can keep. Another strategy incorporated into the privatization program is to sell shares through investment tenders to domestic or foreign investors, where the means of payment would be investment commitments rather than vouchers or cash. In practice, this strategy has amounted to a giveaway of shares to relatives and friends. In other cases, some shares can in principle be retained by the government for some period of time. In yet other cases, the government might contribute the shares toward industry associations and the proposed "financial-industrial groups". In most enterprises, the privatization of the last 20 percent or so of the shares was not fully specified by the privatization plan, and hence shares remain in state hands.

## Developments in Russian privatization

### *Corporatization*

By 1 July 1993, out of 4,972 large enterprises selected for mandatory privatization, GKI and local privatization committees issued decisions to privatize 2,918 enterprises, of which 1,838 were actually registered as joint stock companies. In addition, 6,508 enterprises were corporatized on a voluntarily basis. The apparent enthusiasm for corporatization among many small and medium-sized enterprises suggests that workers and managers find that corporatization gives them more benefits and/or better opportunities to maintain control over the enterprise as compared to small-scale privatization.[3] 1,237 joint stock companies were formed on the basis of subdivisions of state enterprises that previously did not have the status of juridical persons. Overall, by July 1, 1993, 10,663 joint-stock companies were corporatized.

**Table 7.1** Corporatization results by July 1, 1993

| | Mandatory | Voluntary | Subdivisions | Total |
|---|---|---|---|---|
| Permission granted | 2,918 | 6,508 | 1,237 | 10,663 |
| Registered | 1,838 | 4,121 | 518 | 6,477 |
| option 1 (%) | 30.6 | 18.1 | 11.7 | 21.0 |
| option 2 (%) | 68.3 | 80.5 | 87.3 | 77.8 |
| option 3 (%) | 1.1 | 1.4 | 1.0 | 1.3 |

In 78 percent of the enterprises, workers chose the second privatization option, giving them and the managers voting control, whereas in 21 percent, they chose

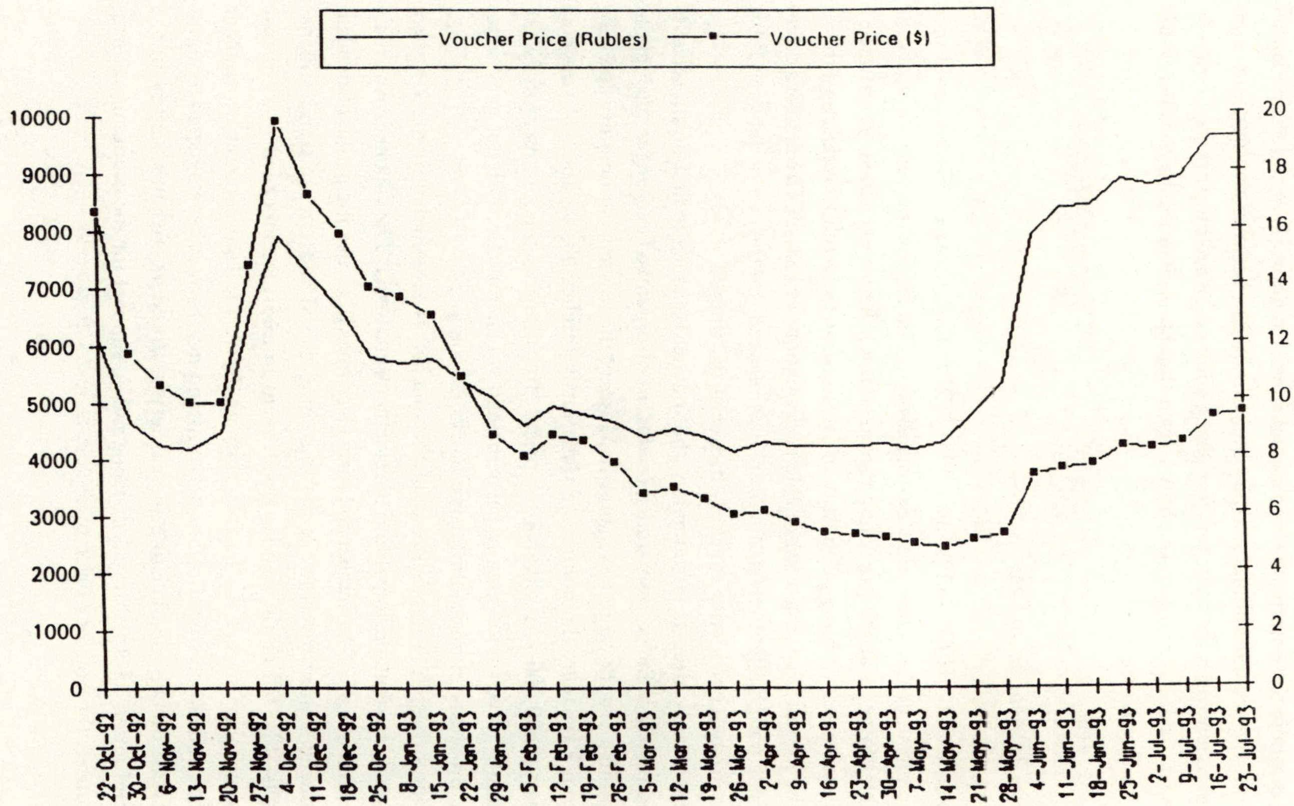


Figure 7.1 Voucher prices: rubles and dollars

the first option. In most cases, the ostensible reason for choosing the second variant is that otherwise control might revert to the outsiders. The first option is chosen in cases where the enterprise is too capital-intensive for workers and their families to afford the second option, or when the relationship between workers and managers is so tense that the managers fear giving voting shares to the workers. Curiously, the third variant is hardly ever chosen, even though it gives the largest ownership stake to the managers.

### *Voucher distribution and use*

Between October 1992 and January 1993, 150 million Russian citizens could pick up their vouchers at their local Savings Banks. The fee for the voucher was only 25 rubles (5 cents at the prevailing exchange rate). As we explained, privatization in Russia was much more populist than privatization in Czechoslovakia, and therefore the idea of charging a reasonable participation fee ($35 in Czechoslovakia) to eliminate marginally interested citizens was rejected. By the end of January 1993, almost 97 percent of the vouchers had been distributed.

Very shortly after its introduction, the voucher became the first liquid security in Russia. It is being actively traded on dozens of organized exchanges throughout the country. On the largest exchange in Moscow, the Russian Commodity and Raw Material Exchange, the volume of trade easily reaches 60,000-100,000 vouchers per day ($600,000 - $1,000,000 at prices prevailing in the summer of 1993). Apparently, investors willing to participate in voucher auctions do not experience major problems in assembling large blocks of vouchers.

Wide swings in the market price of the voucher, as exhibited in Figure 7.1, seem to be easily attributable to political developments in Russia. The voucher rose briefly in the second half of November and early December 1992, in anticipation of demand for vouchers from investors in the upcoming closed subscriptions and voucher auctions. The fall of the Gaidar government in mid-December led to a collapse in the voucher market. In January through April, the large amount of voucher auctions and closed subscriptions notwithstanding, the voucher stagnated in nominal terms, quickly depreciating in real terms. President Yeltsin's victory in the referendum on 25 April revealed strong public support for the economic reform, and caused the voucher price to double in just a few weeks.

**Table 7.2** Voucher auctions by month, December–June 1993

| | Dec | Jan | Feb | March | April | May | June | Total |
|---|---|---|---|---|---|---|---|---|
| Number of enterprises sold | 18 | 105 | 188 | 416 | 582 | 477 | 632 | 2,418 |
| Number of regions participating | 8 | 19 | 29 | 51 | 58 | 48 | 61 | 75 |
| Number of employees (thousands) | 47 | 191 | 181 | 651 | 898 | 511 | 692 | 3,171 |
| Charter capital sold (million rubles) | 513 | 607 | 1,375 | 5,318 | 7,057 | 4,193 | 6,102 | 25,165 |
| Charter capital sold (% weighted average) | 17 | 11 | 23 | 20 | 24 | 21 | 23 | 21 |
| Vouchers accepted (thousands) | 158 | 150 | 501 | 2,188 | 4,854 | 2,666 | 3,526 | 14,043 |
| Auction rate (1,000-ruble shares per voucher, weighted average) | 3.2 | 4 | 2.7 | 2.4 | 1.5 | 1.6 | 1.7 | 1.8 |

**Table 7.3** Voucher auctions by size of enterprise

| Size class | No. of enterprises | % of enterprises | No. of employees (million) | % of employees | Auction rate (weighted average) | No. of employees in Russian industry (million) | % of employees in Russian industry | % privatized |
|---|---|---|---|---|---|---|---|---|
| <500 | 1,354 | 56.0 | 0.28 | 8.9 | 2.5 | 3.02 | 15.0 | 9.3 |
| 501–1,000 | 365 | 15.1 | 0.25 | 7.9 | 1.6 | 2.35 | 11.7 | 10.6 |
| 1,001–5,000 | 584 | 24.2 | 1.23 | 38.6 | 2.1 | 7.28 | 36.2 | 16.8 |
| 5,001–10,000 | 78 | 3.2 | 0.54 | 17.0 | 2.4 | 3.14 | 15.6 | 17.2 |
| >10,000 | 37 | 1.5 | 0.88 | 27.6 | 1.8 | 4.32 | 21.5 | 20.3 |
| Total | 2,418 | 100.0 | 3.17 | 100.0 | 1.8 | 20.11 | 100.0 | 15.8 |

*The pace of voucher auctions*

Voucher auctions began in December 1992, when 18 firms were sold in 8 regions. By April, the pace of sales reached 582 enterprises in 58 regions. In May, the rate of sales fell because people wanted to wait out the April referendum. In June, sales recovered to 632 firms in 61 regions, which seems to be a sustainable monthly rate. Altogether, 2,669 firms have been privatized in voucher auctions by the end of June. Table 7.2 presents some basic statistics on the pace of voucher auctions in Russia.[4]

One way to look at the pace of sales is to focus on the number of employees who work in privatized companies. By the end of June, over 3.6 million employees worked in firms privatized through voucher auctions, which represents roughly 18 percent of the manufacturing labor force in Russia. In March through June the privatization "pace" averaged 700,000 employees per month, or about 3.5 percent of manufacturing employment. If this rate continues to the end of 1993, another 4 million Russian industrial workers will end up in the private sector, so that the total will amount to about 40 percent of manufacturing employment. This is a rather rapid rate for one year of privatization in a country where no other reform has worked.

An average firm that goes through a voucher auction has about 1,300 employees and 50 mn rubles in charter capital. It sells about 22 percent of its shares (11 mn rubles of charter capital) in the auction in exchange for about 5,300 vouchers.

In terms of numbers, medium-sized firms dominate: 71 percent of firms privatized through voucher auctions have less than 1,000 employees. However, large firms account for a very large share of privatized assets and employment. Firms with more than 1,000 employees account for 83 percent of employment and 86 percent of assets of enterprises privatized through voucher auctions. As Table 7.3 suggests, large firms on average privatize somewhat faster than medium and small firms.

## Conclusion: What will happen in the future?

While Russian privatization is off to a fast start, it still faces quite a few obstacles. As of July 1993, the indomitable Russian Parliament is still trying to stop privatization. Several conservative members of the government, while endorsing privatization in principle, are constantly trying to change the program to make it effectively non-viable, and to preserve the existing framework of control over firms. The latest idea is to set up "financial-industrial groups", which are essentially reconstructed industrial ministries. Unfortunately, despite its early success, the ubiquitous Russian bureaucrats are still capable of killing privatization.

Even if privatization succeeds, there is still a long road to restructuring. Privatized firms need appropriate governance structures to be efficient. While in many Russian companies large investors are taking significant stakes, managers and workers still control most firms. It remains to be seen whether this ownership structure is consistent with effective restructuring.

Equally important is that privatized firms need capital to restructure. In the regime of very rapid inflation, commercial banks are not extending long-term loans to viable enterprises. The Central Bank and the government are still extending massive loans and subsidies to both private and public firms, although their choice of firms is usually political rather than economic. The G-7 countries have agreed on a program for providing some investment to privatized Russian firms, although the amounts are unlikely to be large enough to turn the Russian economy around. The genuine restructuring is likely to come from privatization only when the capital problem is solved, which must await monetary stabilization.

In summary, privatization has already begun to bear fruit in terms of restructuring, but the process is not likely to be fast. However painfully, Russian firms are nonetheless moving in the right direction.

## Notes

1. Some of the details of this program are described in Chubais and Vishnevskaya (1993), Shleifer and Vishny (1992) and Frydman and Rapaczynski (1993).
2. Voucher privatization is discussed in great detail by Boycko, Shleifer and Vishny (1993b). Boycko and Shleifer (1993) outline the Russian voucher program.
3. In small-scale privatization in Russia, the main benefit provided to workers is a cash payment equalling 30 percent of the price obtained in the auction. If the workers' collective happens to win the auction, workers receive a 30 percent discount.
4. Voucher auctions remain the best documented part of the large scale privatization in Russia. Little aggregate information exists about the actual pace of closed subscriptions where workers and managers buy shares at fixed prices according to the variant of privatization that they have chosen. But one can safely assume that in the vast majority of cases a closed subscription precedes a voucher auction for a given company. Thus, before a voucher auction, some 40–51 percent of the shares of a typical company have already been sold.

## References

Boycko, Maxim and Andrei Shleifer (1993) in Åslund, Anders and Richard Layard, eds., *Changing the Economic System in Russia*, Pinter, London.

Boycko, Maxim, Andrei Shleifer, and Robert W. Vishny (1993) "Voucher Privatization" *Journal of Financial Economics*, (forthcoming).

Chubais, Anatoly and Maria Vishnevskaya (1993) in Åslund, Anders and Richard Layard, eds., *Changing the Economic System in Russia*, Pinter, London.

Frydman, Roman, Andrzej Rapaczynski, John S. Earle, et al (1993) *The Privatization Process in Russia, Ukraine and the Baltic States*, Central European University Press, London.

Shleifer, Andrei and Robert W. Vishny (1992) "Privatization in Russia: First Steps", mimeo.

# 8 State Enterprises During Transition: Forming Strategies for Survival

*Irina Boeva and Tatiana Dolgopiatova*

This paper is part of a project monitoring the economic conduct of Russian enterprises. The project began in the autumn of 1992. It aims at establishing reactions on the microeconomic level caused by recent changes in both economic policy and the economic system, that is, how state enterprises adapt to the essentially new conditions. The present report discusses enterprises' real survival strategies, as revealed in the course of empirical research. Our study is based on surveys and interviews with managers of industrial enterprises. Ten deep informal interviews (case studies) were made in the period December 1992 – March 1993 at Russian enterprises.[1] All these industrial enterprises have 200–1,200 employees – most have 500–600 employees – and are medium-sized or relatively small by Russian standards.

## Strategies for survival

The analysis has revealed that today the very notion of "survival" has different meanings to different state enterprise directors. The overwhelming majority of the managers consider preserving the work force and maintaining the level of earnings as primary goals. However, some managers see their first aim as stabilizing production and strengthening the position of their enterprise on the market. But usually these intentions are only measures to reach the same main aim – to keep their employees. Only one director defined enterprise survival as having a solid, stable financial position, enabling it to avoid bankruptcy and to develop further.

The priorities of enterprises in spending their financial resources confirm their approach to the notion of "survival". Their top priorities were formed last year:

primarily to increase salaries and to preserve the labour force. Enterprise managers try to raise salaries by all means, despite limited resources. The second major goal is the construction of housing for employees. As far as possible, enterprises invest resources in housing all the time. One director pointed out that all resources, after current costs had been deducted, were being invested in the construction of housing.

Preference is given to current aims in resource use, but the second choice is minor (short-term) investment in the re-equipment and modernization of production, which does not require big investments and which guarantees quick improvements in output (efficiency). Resources are generally spent on small items that give a large effect, such as the production of new commodities, technological improvements or small consignments of equipment. Although these investments are too small to boost aggregate investment, they provide structural changes in production, mostly through changes of the output mix. At some enterprises, partial reconstruction is being carried out. In comparison with the beginning of 1992, managers generally devote more resources to such short-term investments, and at some enterprises such investments will be carried out even to the detriment of dividends, according to their directors.

Available resources are insufficient for investment projects on a large or medium scale. Almost all the directors consider that these projects can be carried out only with the help of foreign investors or the state.

Our case studies have shown that enterprises use different methods to survive. Some of these methods are auxiliary, leading only to partial improvements. Let us look at four examples:

1. Some enterprises possess substantial stocks of raw materials, other materials, and equipment, which were purchased as reserves at the former low fixed prices. Such "fat" enables enterprises to work calmly and with low costs. If an enterprise faces financial difficulties it can always sell these superfluous inventories. For example, one of the enterprises sold off excess vehicles, but kept inventories of oil products "for a rainy day".
2. Enterprises join various "vertical" structures or corporate groups that are reorganized branch structures or new organizations. Most of these enterprises are members of two or three such associations, concerns, or corporations. Usually they help in supply and sales, set up economic links with other Commonwealth states, and organize their own financial institutions which give member enter-

prises credits and financial help on favourable conditions. Moreover, these enterprise organizations are instruments of lobbying, pressuring the government and the Central Bank in order to obtain subsidies, cheap credits and other benefits.

3. Enterprises also join different "horizontal" groups of state enterprises in order to carry out joint strategies. Joint-stock companies, partnerships for investment and production projects are popular forms. Amalgamations are also set up according to the technological chain "supplier-manufacturer-consumer". They establish economic links, pursue coordinated price policy or a policy of mutual restraint, or remove bottle-necks in their production. There are also collusions that function like cartels, agreeing on a minimum price level.
4. Another option is "parasitism" on state property. Enterprises are in full control of their territories, buildings, premises, and equipment. They can dispose of them or let them to other state enterprises, cooperatives, new private sector.

There are also more complex survival strategies that provide for the success of an enterprise. Some of these strategies are unique and can only be implemented by one individual enterprise, thanks to its specific products, its position on the market or some other factor. But there are also general strategies, available for everyone, used by an overwhelming majority of enterprises. Our research materials contain three examples of unique survival methods.

1. One enterprise enjoyed an ideal position. It was the exclusive producer of most types of its output, but it had not been included in the state register of monopoly enterprises. Therefore it could raise its profitability (ratio of profit to costs) to several hundred percent.
2. Two enterprises benefited from their type of output, which remains in short supply, while they have stable sale markets, which guarantees a quick turnover of investments. Therefore, these two enterprises could continue with a minimum of adjustment, while keeping up output levels in the whole plant.
3. A third example is the manufacturing of products for export from imported raw materials with improved technology. Thus, a garment factory thrived, thanks to the attractive design of its products, acceptable quality and cheap labour. This enterprise is constantly expanding its production, even increasing the number of employees as well as permanently raising their salaries, compensating losses from inflation.

The most typical strategies today are to participate in privatization and to adapt production and sales to present demand. In addition, there is adaptation to changes in pricing policy and partly to financial restrictions.

## Privatization

All the directors interviewed, with one exception, agreed that the state ownership of their enterprises had become outdated, especially since it no longer gave any advantages. They could not count on any state financing, and the enterprises have been abandoned by the state.

The processes of setting up joint-stock companies and privatization are treated differently by the directors. Some treat these as a chance to speed up the reforming of their enterprises. Others do not see any difference in principle between setting up a joint-stock company and a lease, considering the conditions of management in both cases to be similar, especially during the first years.

Most of the respondents have similar motives for privatization. The primary motive is to become free, and get away from the power of the bureaucrats. This power is decreasing all the time, but nevertheless the bureaucrats, from the local administration as well as from the corresponding federal department, "are always tempted to lead and control", without understanding the essence of the problems. Another motive is that the employees can purchase an enterprise for a trifle, giving the managers additional opportunities to control or dispose of the property.

The sphere of potential economic decisions is also expanding, involving issues such as the definition of an enterprise's character as well as the formation of enterprise funds. Both the grounds of an enterprise and its capital assets can be used as the management thinks best (if the shareholders do not object). For example, the property can be leased, sold, or invested as a share in the authorized capital of other joint-stock companies. Although the directors emphasize the importance of independence, some think it necessary that the state should provide support, (in the form of investments, favourable credits, or guarantees to foreign investors) to concrete projects of all enterprises, regardless of their ownership status.

Privatization also facilitates the reorganization of internal management and corporate structures, as well as the development of different forms of horizontal amalgamations of enterprises.

Attracting foreign investors is also an important motive for privatization. Foreign investors prefer to work with privatized enterprises. Privatization also makes it possible to attract financial resources from new commercial structures, though most of the managers are not yet ready for this. But some directors would already like to get involved in cooperation with big famous companies, and they are trying to do this, realizing that they have no other sources of finance for development.

Some of the managers also hope that privatization can stimulate a change of attitude among the employees towards their work. But most of the directors, either in leased or already privatized enterprises, have no illusions about the benefits of these "proprietary feelings". Increased pressure on enterprise management to obtain higher salaries or dividends is a more likely result. One of the directors pointed out that if an enterprise becomes a joint-stock company it turns into "a collective farm", which makes it more difficult to take firm decisions and get involved in long-term projects. But the efficiency of decision-making may improve in privatized enterprises in the future, if the ownership is redistributed from the employees to outsiders, who can set up a supervisory board that would control management.

Though the idea of privatization is supported unanimously, the State Privatization Program for 1993 is not supported unconditionally. Some of the directors criticize it, mostly for its excessive regulation and inflexible models. It is quite natural that the managers especially dislike the mandatory establishment of joint-stock companies of open type, because it limits both their power and wealth. Instead, these directors want to let their employees decide what type of joint-stock company that should be set up.

Despite this criticism the directors want to speed up the privatization process. All their complaints about the actual course of privatization centre on the delays and external organizational obstacles. Typical strictures concern the impediments raised by regional authorities, such as procrastination and bureaucracy in the approval of privatization permits.

Most of the enterprises have chosen the second, "more cautious" model of privatization as which allows the employees to preserve control over the enterprise. Two enterprises chose the first model. The directors fear the third model, since it can cause a split among employees.[2] As one of the directors put it, "we are still up to our neck in socialism".

Three of the studied enterprises have already been leased to their employees and are on their way to setting up closed joint-stock companies, in which the shares are distributed among the employees. The possibility of getting employees to invest their personal savings is also being considered. One enterprise had been privatized since autumn 1992. At first, the management of this factory distributed an initial block of shares to the employees. In addition, all the employees got equal opportunity to borrow from the factory's loan counter (at 60 percent interest for half a year) and guarantees, if they wanted to borrow from the State Savings Bank. Then it began to bring in cash from employees in exchange for extra shares issued for an expansion of the working capital. On the whole the employees refused to buy shares, but a group of 12–15 people (mainly managers and 2–3 workers) did buy, becoming the owners of one-third of the shares. As the managing director put it, this group will be capable of pursuing a rather firm policy of limiting dividends, while supporting investments in production, which will enable the enterprise to undertake substantial re-equipping in the near future.

## Sales strategies

Now practically all enterprises have understood the importance of sales activities, and they have begun to work out their line of conduct on the market. Many have already been forced to choose their tactics, since they are faced with excessive stocks of their products as well as a sharp fall in demand for them. However, not all enterprises have started considering what kind of sales strategies they should pursue.

An easy change that many enterprises attempt is to try to change the output mix. Several enterprises which manufactured industrial products are now beginning to manufacture consumer goods. Some producers of industrial products are developing the next step downstream in that line of production. For example, a producer of ferro-concrete structures has begun organizing its own contract construction works. When reorganizing output mix, the enterprises have begun to orient themselves to possible consumers, whom they had completely ignored in the previous socialist economy.

When choosing customers, the directors are guided by several considerations. First of all they try to deal directly with the final consumer. Then, they orient themselves to solvent customers, who can pay in advance or at the moment of purchase. At present, it is convenient for every enterprise to have clients who pay cash.

Only a few respondents had worked out long-term strategies for the choice of customers. For long-term cooperation, enterprises are still focusing upon state (or former state) structures which are well-established on the market. One of the enterprises studied had redirected its sales. Previously, its main customer was a big

Moscow enterprise, but it did not make any progress in adapting to the market. Today this enterprise sells primarily to another big, former state enterprise in Latvia, which has now been privatized, and which has been successful in developing a market not only at home, but also in Russia. Since they are orienting their production to long-term contacts with their customers, the directors have begun to pay attention not only to their counterparts' present financial state, but also to their long-term perspectives on the market: their competitiveness, presence of advanced technical policy, perspectives of production and market expansion. Sometimes an enterprise has a long-term collaboration with a customer that is a trading company, but such a company requires a thorough evaluation of the stability of its activities and perspectives.

A group of enterprises are being forced to reduce their output, but nevertheless they try to avoid severe cuts, preserving capacities and keeping leading specialists. They are assuming that the consumers of these products – insolvent at present – will be privatized and improve their financial situation, or that the state will again finance activities such as construction, repairing roads, or repairing and replacing spare parts of military equipment. Also other CIS states which do not produce these spare parts may be future customers. Then the traditional products will be salable again.

Enterprises must search for new customers and develop new markets. The search for new markets takes several forms. Some managers seek new customers on their own – as a rule through other directors within their own circle. Sometimes very cautiously and through acquaintances, they establish contacts with "commercial structures", as the new trading companies are called.[3]

To us, the most interesting phenomenon is close cooperation with these new companies on the market. In one case a trading company sells a part of the enterprise's products, mostly new consumer goods, while the enterprise itself sells its traditional products through its old channels. In addition, the industrial enterprise may turn to the trading enterprise when difficulties arise, such as in obtaining new types of inputs, imported raw materials, and raw materials from other CIS states. The directors who are involved in such cooperation reckon that the new "commercial structures" know the demands and the prices of the market better. Therefore they can help an industrial enterprise to organize its sales in a more profitable way. However, other directors complained of fraud on the part of both suppliers and consumers from new "commercial structures" (especially from small enterprises).

Another tactic for selling products under the current conditions of decreasing domestic demand is to go into the international market, but this is only an option for a few. Such enterprises must have an acceptably high level of production technology. Export sales also presuppose comparatively low labour costs. In addition, enterprises that are involved in one way or another in international trade in raw materials can combine this with some trade in its own semi-manufactured products.

For many state enterprises, competition has become a reality. After having felt the limitations of the demand side, they are forced to seek ways of raising the competitiveness of their products.

Practically all the directors have understood the necessity of price competition: the better opportunity an enterprise has to keep its prices at an average level or even lower, the greater are its chances to achieve sufficient and stable sales. That is why most of the directors are making efforts to reduce production costs. Enterprises are trying to economize on different expenses, such as the cost of raw materials and other materials and various fixed costs. It is very difficult for the directors to economize on the wage fund because of social and political pressures. Furthermore, some managers cannot accept this for ideological reasons. So far, the managers are trying to reduce costs without cutting employee benefits.

Very few enterprises are trying to raise the competitiveness of their output by improving the quality of their products or by introducing new ranges of products, though many of them understand that this would be an effective measure. It requires capital investment, sometimes of significant size, but at present few enterprises have sufficient funds for serious investment.

The problem of finding solvent purchasers has brought competition to Russia's industrial producers, but there are remaining obstacles to free, honest competition and several of them will grow stronger. One problem is the heavy monopolization. Production in the USSR was rather monopolized, but it has been reinforced in two waves in the course of the reforms. The first wave came with the disintegration of the USSR, when many enterprises that were not monopolists in the USSR became monopolists in Russia. The second wave was caused when many enterprises decreased the volumes of production, as a response to industrial chaos, inflation, financial instability and so on, either because they could not adapt themselves sufficiently or as a defensive tactic. As a result numerous enterprises have become producers of shortage products.

It is noteworthy that such monopolists conduct themselves differently. Some enterprises understand that their monopolies are temporary and take advantage of the shortage by earning money to invest in machinery and equipment, in increasing the technological level of their production, in moving into new ranges of products and in developing new markets. Others, with a lower technological level, simply enjoy the monopoly profits, spending them on the employees' well-being, without thinking about the future. Enterprises in the military-industrial complex, which are relatively high-tech but are having difficulties with their traditional sales, can quickly go over to producing some simple civilian products, when they realize that this can be profitable. Many have already done so.

## Foreign economic activity

All enterprises display a steadily growing interest in foreign economic activity, but most of the directors remain rather sceptical for various reasons. One director expressed the opinion that substantial capital investments from Western businessmen and interest in joint development of advanced production in Russia were not expected, because of political motives, such as "nobody needs a strong Russia". But scepticism is mostly caused by the following factors:

1. Foreign economic activity is unprofitable because of the present legislation. A share of foreign trade revenues must be allocated to the state currency reserve and enterprises must exchange half the currency revenues for rubles.
2. Because of the low technological level of Russian factories, Russian goods are not very competitive. A sufficient amount of capital investments, primarily in hard currency, will be required to solve this problem.
3. Industrial enterprises lack the necessary contacts to enter external markets directly, since state foreign trade organizations formerly had a complete monopoly on foreign economic activity. The establishment of contacts with foreign enterprises is proceeding slowly. Industrial enterprises do not want to sell their products through foreign trade associations any longer, because they lose a lot in this way, since these associations are used to behaving like monopolists, refusing to transfer their contacts to the producing enterprises. Enterprises have never had the contacts nor the experience of foreign trade.

While some enterprises have adopted a sceptical view of foreign trade activities, taking a passive position and marking time, others are trying to find a way out.

Usually, Russian industrial products cannot be sold directly on the external market because of low competitiveness. Therefore, Russian enterprises try to organize joint production. Most of the respondents have pursued negotiations rather actively, but their results have not been very impressive. Joint production has only been organized at one out of the ten enterprises investigated.

The schemes of joint production are rather diverse. Many Russian enterprises try to set up joint production with foreign partners; these partners contribute hard currency for capital investments, for the re-equipment of the production apparatus, and for foreign technology. Foreign companies have shown interest in such schemes, but they are waiting and in reality little has happened. Foreign partners are wary of political instability and the instability of legislation.

Some directors consider foreign economic cooperation in Russia to be unprofitable, and they try to organize joint production in another country, typically a Third World country, where producing the same type of products, usually industrial goods, is competitive. In some cases enterprises simply try to sell their finished products abroad. Defence enterprises in particular are now trying to sell armaments, equipment and spare parts for Russian machinery directly to Third World countries.

## Pricing policy

The liberalization of prices presented state enterprises with the problem of forming their own pricing strategies. The majority of enterprises apply the principle of cost-plus pricing (actual costs plus a "normal" mark-up as a percentage of costs). Stable inflationary expectations have made plant managers adopt inflexible price tactics. Even if solvent demand is not sufficient, they usually do not reduce prices. Either they continue turning out products that end up in warehouses or slow down until the price level is regarded as acceptable. Deliveries to "friends" can be continued without prepayment, which increases inter-enterprise arrears. In reality, newly-granted credits lead to a rise in wages and expand solvent demand, which in turn leads to a boost of sales. This also spurs inflation and signs of panic buying appear from time to time, which causes a new growth in expenses and then in prices. The stereotype price behavior that results is ultimately based on enterprises' confidence about obtaining cheap credits and other state aid, and should not be regarded as a simple manifestation of monopoly.

Another reason for inflexible price policies is that enterprises are sometimes incapable of feeling the level of demand for their products immediately, especially for new product lines, because they are not the beneficiaries of additional revenues which tend to go to various intermediaries.

Still, some pricing trends result from monopolies on some markets. Various cartel agreements between manufacturers have become widespread. One type of agreement is restraining prices within a chain of interrelated production, so that the end product, which often goes to the final consumer or to foreign markets, can be competitive. Such agreements can be informal and connected with permanent links between enterprises. They are both more frequent and lasting in concerns and associations which have agreed upon acceptable price levels in advance.

Another type of monopolistic agreement, which tends not to be revealed, is the establishment of a minimum price for a given commodity by a group of manufacturers who dominate the regional or Russian market. For example, in one region all lumbering enterprises agreed on the minimum permissible prices of their output.

An additional evidence of monopoly of the Russian economy is the widespread practice of discriminatory pricing. Three levels of prices on one and the same product are established by the manufacturers, and relate to different categories of customers. Enterprises reserve the lowest level of prices for their narrow circle of traditional customers. These prices cover expenses and ensure the producers of a modest profit. As a part of this strategy, some enterprises, well aware of the financial standing of their steady customers, set the price that each customer can "afford". Prices for new or occasional partners – state enterprises – are usually set at higher level, but below the prices charged to non-state customers. Prices for these customers are the highest, but still below the prices at Russian commodity exchanges.

Price discrimination arises from plant managers adhering to their old links and their specific attitude toward the non-state sector. Hidden barter trade – mutual deliveries at lower prices – is also a form of price discrimination. Its causes range from the curtailing of expenses or tax avoidance to supplying employees with foodstuffs. This great variety of ulterior motives cannot be explained simply by the goal of maximizing profits, even though economic theory tells us that the profit motive underlies the phenomenon of price discrimination on a monopolistic market.

## Partial adaptation to financial restrictions

The majority of enterprises have been hit by a shortage of current assets. To some this is a continuing hardship, severely crippling their performance, while others face it only periodically, but with likely adverse consequences. The insolvency of enterprises is explained both by general economic conditions and by the behavior of each given enterprise. The main causes are the continuing devaluation of current assets due to high inflation, the shrinking of markets, stocks of unused raw materials, stocks of unsold goods in warehouses and in workshops, and large debts owed to enterprises by customers.

When an enterprise has no money in its bank account, its managers tend to view the situation as a temporary difficulty, instead of an indication of their financial unsoundness. To them, the fact that they have run out of bank money does not necessarily mean that they have no funds. Therefore, when interviewed, they keep citing figures of debts owed to them by their customers, obviously deeming them recoverable. One manager, while complaining about the lack of funds to repair equipment at his plant, stressed: "It's not that we have no money, it's just that we have no money in our bank account!"

At many enterprises, managers are trying to blame the existing financial difficulties on the government and the banking system. Some of their demands are reasonable, such as improvements in the payment procedures and in interstate settlements. At the same time, they are appealing to the government to introduce the indexation of current assets, to enforce settlement crediting of debt servicing between enterprises, and to grant soft credits. The impression is that such appeals are rather "automatic" and that enterprise managers make them just in case, to be on the safe side. Generally, managers realize that the measures they urge the government to take can only bring short-lived relief, after which things will get even worse. But still, to the majority of managers, their own difficulties outweigh such adversities as inflation, though their concern about the latter is growing.

Enterprises are using various means to overcome their financial difficulties. They are struggling to stabilize payments and settlements. Prepayment is increasingly coming into practice, and now transactions with customers are often based on prepayment schemes. But deliveries to traditional customers and troubled state-owned enterprises can sometimes be made on credit: a manager of such an enterprise is usually taken at his word. Private companies or cooperatives are dealt with cautiously, and any delivery to them requires prepayment, but even so fraud takes place occasionally.

To accelerate and stabilize their turnover of money, enterprises are forced to reject economic ties with other former Soviet republics, particularly with Ukraine. They are breaking well-established business contacts and shifting to Russian partners, for fear of losses through devaluations of the currencies of the other republics.

Many enterprises have to use short-term bank credits, although interest rates are often considered outrageous.[4] Other managers abstain from such credits on principle. Sometimes credits are provided by customers. For example, a contractor engaged to execute construction work and to furnish equipment to oil producers may be given a very soft credit for the work to be done.

In some cases, enterprises exchange goods under a mutual redemption scheme in order "to economize" current assets. This sort of barter is widely practiced by enterprises with a broad range of output and no bank money. An example is an enterprise producing building materials. It obtains timber, delivers wood-working products for a cement plant, and in return it gets cement, which it uses to manufacture slabs for the timber suppliers.[5]

According to industrial managers, their financial potentiality is also limited by taxes. Of course, they all complain of exorbitant taxes. But the main reason for their discontent is their being placed in the same tax-paying category as traders and middlemen. They are jealous of the newly-formed private and semi-private sector and the high salaries of those engaged in it. Many managers interviewed deem it necessary to exempt industrial enterprises' investments from taxes and offer them financial privileges.

The majority of managers do not conceal that they have learned to dodge taxes. They say that they mainly use legal loopholes, but they do not reveal the technicalities. Still, some of the tricks they use can be surmised: most probably, they declare lower-than-market values on goods because their customers have provided raw materials, they under-report and invoice production figures and cash sales are not recorded, and prices for mutual deliveries have been set below market prices. The latter method is very popular and has been adopted in barter transactions. In fact, such barter is motivated by the wish to evade taxes. One enterprise selling 5 percent of its products in this way even keeps accountants in charge of such operations. Interestingly, in this case, the state-owned enterprises behave in quite the same manner as private ones, to whom tax evasion is a normal practice.

Economic reforms have limited the financial "freedom" of enterprises. However, at present credit policy is not very tight, since credits are available at market rates that do not correspond to inflation, and they are also available at "soft" rates, though to obtain them an enterprise has to "press and beg". Privileges and subsidies are not granted to all: some enterprises are forced to face the tough market realities, while others, patronized by regional authorities, or belonging to a certain industrial sector or benefiting from other advantages, enjoy better credit regimes. Some support can also be provided through old informal connections, through incorporation into vertical intra-branch structures or through consolidation with the banking system.

The contradictory behavior of the state-owned enterprises is determined, on the one hand, by the shortness of the period of tight stabilization and, on the other hand, by the unusual financial problems that the enterprises have faced. For one purpose, enterprises are eliciting new concessions and privileges from the government, for another aim, they try to find their own ways to obtain financial stability. This can hardly be called financial responsibility. As previously, enterprises pin their hopes on some loosening of financial constraints, on governmental backing, privileges, and subsidies. At the same time, changes in their attitudes to financial resources and their way of managing these resources can be noted. Enterprises have felt a need for money. A common expression by managers was: "once you have it, you can buy whatever you need!"

An important observation is that when financial constraints come into effect, an adaptation of production is induced. This financial impact often governs decision-making, which was impossible under the old system of state enterprise management.

Both production and distribution are changing structurally, becoming more oriented towards profits, towards increasing turnover and more stable sales. There is a noticeable tendency to move to the production of consumer commodities and a propensity for entering the consumer market with both traditional and new products. Furthermore, the enterprises are engaged in acquiring new regional markets and are looking for new customers, such as non-state commercial structures.

Operational management of enterprises also involves financial concerns. In deciding what customer to supply, what to produce, and who should make prepayment, the managers have to consider their financial standing.

The process of price formation is not explicitly linked to these financial issues. Usually, prices do not fall even when demand is low. For one commodity, prices are stable; for another, the producer intends to reduce production and to change the range of products. As a rule, enterprises do their best to maintain prices and wait until the crisis is over, because the market improves periodically as a result of credit injections and inflationary expectations.

Employment policy is not yet much influenced by the financial constraints. Although some managers realize the necessity of reducing their work force, jobs are generally preserved, and most dismissals take place in research and development or information departments. More common alternatives to dismissals are reduced working hours, the offer of vacations, the switch of workers to jobs such as tidying up plant grounds. Forced dismissals because of redundancy are very rare. Presumably, managers wait until workers themselves choose to quit but try to avoid conflicts.

At the same time, numerous financial difficulties make enterprises rebound outside of the financial sphere. Forms of such "extra-financial" benefits are the supply of goods without prepayment and the selective allocation of credits to traditional customers, cash sales of products, deliveries under reciprocal debt-servicing schemes, barter and so forth. Characteristically, such transactions have become particularly popular, when the credit and monetary policy have been tight. Such are the enterprises' responses to the efforts of the government to improve money circulation.

## Summary

In conclusion, we would like to stress that the new strategies of enterprises have been caused by new conditions and are a symptom of them moving toward a market economy. But the strategies are mixed. Among these new strategies there is a traditional line of conduct, with calls for state support, which is predominant at some enterprises. Enterprises still hope, and still try to pressure the government and other authorities to offer financial benefits and support. Today, the directors' particular interpretation of "survival" indicates we should view the economic behaviour of most state enterprises as a reflection of a special form of "partial labour property," combined with an orientation to state paternalism.

## Notes

1. Seven were located in Moscow, one in Tatarstan, one in Vologda, and one in Tiumen oblast.
2. See Chapter 7 for an explanation of the three models of privatization. (Ed.)
3. Current Russian label for all kinds of new trading companies, both private and semi-state enterprises, small as well as large. (Ed.)
4. But the real interest rate is negative. (Ed.)
5. Barter also implies an indexation of payments. (Ed.)

# 9 The Conditions of Life

*Andrei Illarionov, Richard Layard and Peter Orszag**

## Introduction

The Western media often depict the average Russian as starving and destitute. This is of course absurd. But hardship has increased since the reform for a substantial portion of the population. Average living standards have fallen and inequality has increased. How much? We begin by documenting the changes as accurately as possible, showing what is true and what is exaggerated.

In Part 2, we ask why it has happened. Why have real wages fallen and why has wage dispersion increased? We find that economic forces explain much of the story. And how have pensions and family benefits adjusted? The social safety net, though well-organized, has left many large families poor. The problem of poor children is much more serious than the problem of poor pensioners.

In Part 3, we look at unemployment – tomorrow's economic and social problem. We note how inflation has eroded the value of unemployment benefits and also outline an appropriate employment policy framework to cope with the unemployment problem as it unfolds.

Finally, in Part 4, we look at the rise in regional inequality, which will be an increasingly important feature of the Russian scene.

## 1 What has happened to living standards?

### *Average income and consumption*

In January 1992, Russia liberalized its prices and they rose immediately by 3.5 times. During the rest of 1992, prices rose again by 7.5 times.

How did living standards respond? The shock of the initial price rise was substantial, but from then on incomes adjusted surprisingly well to the ongoing inflation (with some improvement in standards of living over the year). Our discussion therefore focuses on the average standard of living in the year 1992, though we give details on each quarter in the tables.

We begin with the standard figures on real income and real consumption, which give a very distorted impression. We then go on to explain why they exaggerate the problem. On the standard measures (shown in Table 9.1), real income fell by one-half compared to the previous year and by one-third compared with 1985.[1] The corresponding falls in consumption were 57 and 51 percent.

**Table 9.1** Indices of real income, consumers' expenditure, wages, and pensions (1991=100)

| | Income | Consumers' expenditure | Average wage | Average pension | 'Minimum pension' |
|---|---|---|---|---|---|
| 1985 | 74.5 | 88.5 | 87.3 | 63.1 | 69.5 |
| 1990 | 101.0 | 109.4 | 111.4 | 74.3 | 84.2 |
| 1991 | 100.0 | 100.0 | 100.0 | 100.0 | 100.0 |
| 1992 | 48.7 | 43.3 | 67.7 | 36.6 | 42.4 |
| 1992 Q1 | 42.5 | 42.1 | 59.8 | 32.2 | 44.3 |
| Q2 | 41.7 | 38.2 | 63.3 | 36.6 | 42.1 |
| Q3 | 53.3 | 43.5 | 70.7 | 36.6 | 42.9 |
| Q4 | 57.0 | 49.2 | 76.8 | 41.0 | 40.3 |
| 1993 Q1 | 45.4 | 43.8 | 64.8 | | 35.4 |

*Note*: The table depicts the relevant nominal figure deflated by the Soviet Union retail price index for 1985–90 and the Russian consumer price index for 1991 onwards. The quarterly figures are given on an annual basis.

As the figures in Table 9.1 imply, the savings rate differed dramatically in these years.[2] In 1985, it was 5.7 percent; in 1991, 20.8 percent; and in 1992, 31.3 percent. In 1985 savings were forced up since product markets did not clear due to price controls. But in 1991 and 1992 savings were forced up by inflation, which made it necessary to save in order to maintain the real value of bank balances. In fact, savings were not high enough in either year to avert a fall in the real value of household financial assets.[3]

Clearly consumption is a better measure of welfare than income. But in evaluating the consumers' expenditure figures, however, several important offsetting features must be noted. First, even consumers' expenditure is a misleading guide to the level of welfare because many key services – the most prominent of which is housing – are still heavily subsidized. Thus if money outlays fall by one-half relative to the prices of purchased goods and services, it does not follow that welfare falls by the same proportion. Somewhat more formally, suppose that utility is given by $X_1^{\alpha}X_2^{1-\alpha}$, where the price of $X_2$ is approximately zero. Then if the quantity of purchased goods falls by one-half, utility only falls by roughly $\alpha/2$.[4] Since, in Russia, housing is almost free, as is domestic heating, electricity, gas, telephone, and public transport, $\alpha$ may be as low as 2/3. The fall in welfare has therefore been substantially less than the fall in measured real purchases.

Second, queues have largely disappeared. The value of this change is difficult to measure. Suppose the average adult woman spent 15 hours per week queuing when she would have otherwise been at work (if employed) or at home (if a pensioner). Suppose further that the comparative disutility of queuing were equal on average to one-fifth the average wage.[5] Then the personal utility cost of queuing was at least 5 percent of total income and at least 6 percent of consumers' expenditure in 1985. It is perhaps equally important that people no longer experience constant frustration in searching for goods.

Third, there has been a visible improvement in the quality of services and, in some cases, in the quality of goods.

**Table 9.2** Indices of real consumers' expenditure: measured vs. survey data (1991=100)

| | | Measured consumer' expenditure | Survey data consumers' expenditure |
|---|---|---|---|
| 1991 | | 100.0 | 100.0 |
| 1992 | Q1 | 42.1 | 51.8 |
| | Q2 | 38.2 | 52.8 |
| | Q3 | 43.4 | 74.2 |
| | Q4 | 49.2 | 70.4 |

*Note*: The table presents indices of the relevant nominal figures deflated by the consumer price index. The survey data figures apply only to workers' households.

Fourth, the official statistics fail to reflect unmeasured expenditure. Since expenditure is measured as income minus taxes minus the increase in asset holdings, measured expenditure excludes the impact of unmeasured income – a growing proportion of total income. This is partly offset by the fact that unmeasured asset holdings (e.g., dollars) have also risen. But the overall effect of the measurement problems is probably to bias downward the change in consumers' expenditure. This bias is evident in Goskomstat's survey data on consumers' expenditure (obtained from regular surveys of 49,000 households). This is compared with the measured consumers' expenditure data in Table 9.2. The survey-based consumers' expenditure has fallen significantly less than measured consumers' expenditure. Moreover, by end-1992 the survey figure appeared to exceed the measured figure by some 50 percent.[6]

Finally, consumption of self-produced food, especially potatoes, has increased during the economic reform process. These five considerations strongly suggest that real consumption has fallen less than suggested in Table 9.1.

### *Structure of consumption*

However, there has certainly been some fall in real consumption. A standard indicator of living standards is the share of expenditure spent on food: the poor spend a higher proportion of their income on food than the rich. This is of course a rather crude indicator since it is bound to reflect relative prices as well as real income. However, in the Russian case continuing subsidies to the agro-industry have tended to reduce the relative price of food since the beginning of the reform process (see Figure 9.1). Other things being equal, we would therefore have expected the share of food expenditure to fall.[7] In fact, according to the Goskomstat household budget survey, it rose significantly (see Table 9.3). This seems to confirm a fall in living standards.

The striking thing in the household survey data is that, by the second half of last year, real expenditure on food had recovered to its average 1991 level (see Table 9.4). The real declines were in the consumption of non-food items like clothing and footwear, which were nearly halved, and in expenditures on services like cultural activities and holidays.

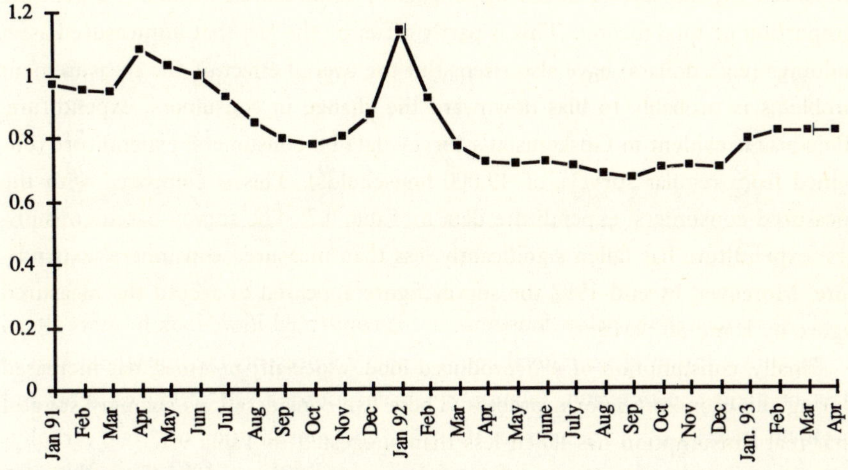


**Figure 9.1** The relative price of food (CPI for foodstuffs/CPI for non-foodstuffs, Dec. 1990=1)
*Note*: The consumer price indices in 1992 (Q4) with 1991=1.0 were as follows: 29.5 (CPI), 24.5 (food), 31.5 (non-food), 23.9 (alcohol), 35.5 (paid services).

**Table 9.3** Expenditure shares

| | | Total | Foodstuffs | Non-foodstuffs | Alcohol | Services |
|---|---|---|---|---|---|---|
| *Workers' households*: | | | | | | |
| 1991 | | 100 | 37 | 49 | 4 | 9 |
| 1991 | December | 100 | 34 | 54 | 3 | 9 |
| 1992 | Q1 | 100 | 45 | 43 | 4 | 8 |
| | Q2 | 100 | 43 | 44 | 3 | 10 |
| | Q3 | 100 | 41 | 48 | 3 | 8 |
| | Q4 | 100 | 44 | 45 | 3 | 7 |
| *Pensioners' households*: | | | | | | |
| 1992 | January | 100 | 71 | 16 | 5 | 8 |
| | April | 100 | 69 | 7 | 5 | 19 |
| | July | 100 | 79 | 10 | 6 | 5 |
| | October | 100 | 78 | 13 | 4 | 6 |

**Table 9.4** Indices of real expenditure (1991=100)

| | | Food | Non-food | Alcohol | Services | Total |
|---|---|---|---|---|---|---|
| *Workers' households:* | | | | | | |
| 1991 | | 100 | 100 | 100 | 100 | 100 |
| 1992 | Q1 | 60 | 44 | 66 | 60 | 52 |
| | Q2 | 69 | 42 | 65 | 56 | 53 |
| | Q3 | 100 | 68 | 70 | 50 | 74 |
| | Q4 | 101 | 61 | 78 | 40 | 70 |

This pattern, by type of consumption, is confirmed if we look in more detail at the consumption of individual goods. Table 9.5 presents the household survey data on food consumption, including consumption of self-produced food and payment in kind. As is clear from the table, the consumption of basic carbohydrates like bread and potatoes did not fall between 1991 and 1992. Even for meat and milk products, the decline in consumption was quite small. The fall in food purchases during the first half of 1992 (see Table 9.4) was significantly offset by consumption of home-produced potatoes and by drawing down other accumulated stocks of food.

**Table 9.5** Consumption of food and food products (kg per person)

| | 1991 | 1992 | 1992 Q1 | Q2 | Q3 | Q4 | 1992/1991 |
|---|---|---|---|---|---|---|---|
| Bread products | 101 | 104 | 26 | 26 | 27 | 26 | 1.03 |
| Potatoes | 98 | 106 | 28 | 26 | 23 | 29 | 1.09 |
| Vegetables and melons | 87 | 78 | 17 | 15 | 25 | 20 | 0.90 |
| Fruits and berries | 35 | 29 | 7 | 4 | 9 | 9 | 0.85 |
| Sugar | 29 | 26 | 6 | 6 | 6 | 8 | 0.91 |
| Meat and meat products | 65 | 58 | 15 | 14 | 13 | 16 | 0.89 |
| Milk and milk products (litres) | 349 | 294 | 62 | 75 | 82 | 75 | 0.84 |
| Fish products | 14 | 12 | 3 | 3 | 3 | 3 | 0.81 |
| Eggs (number) | 229 | 243 | 54 | 72 | 65 | 52 | 1.06 |
| Vegetable oils and other fats | 6 | 7 | 2 | 2 | 2 | 2 | 1.10 |

By comparison, there have been significant falls in purchases of textiles and footwear. These are shown in Table 9.6.

**Table 9.6** Purchases of non-food commodities (per person)

| | 1991 | 1992 | 1992/1991 |
|---|---|---|---|
| Textile material (metres) | 9 | 6 | 0.67 |
| Knitted underclothes | 7 | 5 | 0.66 |
| Socks and stockings (pairs) | 15 | 10 | 0.70 |
| Footwear (pairs) | 8 | 6 | 0.70 |
| Soap (kg) | 4 | 2 | 0.55 |

*Inequality*

Not only has real income fallen; it has also become more unequal. Table 9.8 shows the distribution of individuals according to the per capita income of their family (a "family" is defined as any group of relatives sharing a common budget). The most striking change has been the fall in the income of the poor relative to the average. The lower decile income (i.e., the tenth percentile) is now only 44 percent of the median, compared with 52 percent in 1991.

At the upper decile, we find no substantial increase in inequality relative to the median. However, there has almost certainly been a significant increase in inequality at the very top of the income distribution, which is not analyzed in detail in the published statistics. One should also note that the budget survey, though it covers 49,000 families, tends to under-represent people working in the most rapidly developing parts of the economy (including many of the *nouveaux riches*) as well as people on the margin of society (including those whose incomes have suffered most).[8]

The figures in Table 9.7 represent the distribution of nominal income; three other considerations should in principle be taken into account. First, since relative food prices have fallen and the income elasticity of food consumption is less than one, the true increase in inequality is less than that shown in Table 9.7. Second, goods with extremely low prices (like housing and transportation) were and continue to be distributed more equally than money income, which would also imply that true inequality has grown less than measured income inequality. On the other hand, when there is rationing by queues, true inequality is less than measured inequality in income, because poor people are willing to devote more time to queuing (Polterovich, 1993). Thus the abolition of queues of itself tends to increase inequality. It is not practicable to give a quantitative evaluation of these three factors, but they may tend to cancel out.

**Table 9.7** Income inequality (individual data, monthly per capita income)

| | Upper decile* | Median* | Lower decile* | Upper ductile/ median | Lower ductile/ median | Upper decile/ lower ductile | Gini coefficient |
|---|---|---|---|---|---|---|---|
| 1991 | 333.5 | 183.5 | 96.3 | 1.82 | 0.52 | 3.46 | 0.26 |
| 1992 | | | | | | | |
| January | 154.7 | 88.8 | 49.7 | 1.74 | 0.56 | 3.11 | 0.24 |
| February | 138.2 | 86.1 | 49.1 | 1.61 | 0.57 | 2.82 | |
| March | 146.2 | 87.2 | 49.2 | 1.68 | 0.56 | 2.97 | 0.28 |
| August | 155.3 | 83.8 | 38.6 | 1.85 | 0.46 | 4.03 | 0.30 |
| November | 146.9 | 82.6 | 39.1 | 1.78 | 0.47 | 3.76 | |
| December | 243.9 | 117.5 | 53.8 | 2.08 | 0.46 | 4.53 | 0.33 |
| 1993 | | | | | | | |
| March | 147.6 | 78.4 | 36.8 | 1.88 | 0.47 | 4.02 | 0.32 |
| April | 122.8 | 67.4 | 29.8 | 1.82 | 0.44 | 4.12 | 0.32 |

*Notes*: * Rubles, December 1990 prices.

Many discussions of inequality in Russia point to the high proportion of people who can barely afford to purchase meat. Yet the data show that this was so even before the reform. Inequality of meat consumption increased only marginally in 1992 (see Table 9.8).

**Table 9.8** Distribution of per capita consumption of meat (kg per month)

| | Upper decile | Median | Lower decile | Upper decile/ median | Lower decile/ median | Upper decile/ lower decile |
|---|---|---|---|---|---|---|
| 1991 | 6.3 | 2.7 | 1.0 | 2.33 | 0.37 | 6.30 |
| 1992 | 6.5 | 2.7 | 0.9 | 2.41 | 0.33 | 7.22 |

So how does inequality in Russia compare with that in the West? This is a difficult question, which was a principal focus of the book by Atkinson and Micklewright (1992) on inequality in the pre-reform period. For the United Kingdom, they give data on the distribution of individuals in 1985 by household income per capita as follows:[9]

**Table 9.9** Income inequality in the United Kingdom and Russia (individual data, monthly per capita income)

| | | Upper decile/lower decile | Gini coefficient |
|---|---|---|---|
| United Kingdom | 1985 | 3.8 | 0.30 |
| Russia | December 1992 | 4.5 | 0.33 |
| | April 1993 | 4.1 | 0.32 |

Given the point made earlier about free services, one can probably conclude that income inequality in Russia is still no greater than in the UK. This is of course substantially less than in the United States.

## *Who are the poor?*

The main policy issue is the well-being of those at the bottom end of the income scale. Indeed, it is crucial for policy purposes to identify the groups which have the highest incidence of poverty. To examine this issue, Goskomstat is undertaking, in collaboration with the World Bank, a longitudinal study of some 7,000 households. This is intended to be a more representative sample than the household budget survey. The income of each individual is then compared with a minimum subsistence level of income established by the Ministry of Labor. The subsistence standard differs with age and starts from FAO/WHO estimates of the diet an average individual would need in order to maintain body weight at a satisfactory level of activity (which is necessarily a somewhat subjective concept). This is increased by one standard deviation of the distribution of individual differences in need. It is then augmented further to account for non-food purchases, making food account (on average) for 68 percent of total expenditure. Table 9.10 shows the calculated subsistence level for the average person and the average pensioner:[10]

**Table 9.10** Minimum subsistence level per person, 1992 (R/month)

| | Average person | Older adults | 'Minimum pension' (x1.2) |
|---|---|---|---|
| February | 686 | 468 | 410 |
| April | 1,016 | 700 | 650 |
| June | 1,344 | 926 | 1,080 |
| August | 1,868 | 1,381 | 1,584 |
| September | 2,147 | 1,561 | 1,584 |
| October | 2,763 | 1,990 | 1,584 |
| November | 3,450 | 2,464 | 2,700 |

*Notes*: *Males over 60, females over 55.

Using this standard, it is possible to address the question of poverty.[11] The proportion of people living in poverty in each group in society in July-September 1992 is shown in Table 11. The results are striking and somewhat surprising.[12] One-half of Russia's children live in poverty. This compares with 37 percent of all Russians. Elderly women are no more likely to be poor than the population at large, and elderly men are less likely.[13]

**Table 9.11** Percentage of individuals living below the poverty level

| | % |
|---|---|
| Total population | 37 |
| Children 0–6 | 46 |
| Children 7–15 | 47 |
| Young adults | 36 |
| Females 31–54 | 35 |
| Males 31–60 | 34 |
| Females 55+ | 34 |
| Males 60+ | 22 |
| Families with: 3 or more children* | 72 |
| 2 children | 47 |
| 1 child | 34 |
| Families with a single parent* | 55 |
| with an unemployed member | 45 |
| with a disabled member | 45 |
| with an elderly person | 31 |

*Notes*: * In Russia, there are 0.8 million families with 3 or more children and 2.4 million

The most severe incidence of poverty is among families with three or more children, families with a single parent, and families with an unemployed or disabled member. Only 19 percent of poor households are headed by an elderly person (often living on their own). This raises policy issues to which we return later.

## 2 Why the changes?

What explains the pattern of incomes described in Part 1? The family depends on its wage income, if any, and on the social safety net. We begin with wages.

### *Average wages*

The measured real wage (the average wage divided by the price level) in 1992 was one-third lower than in 1991, and nearly a quarter lower than in 1985. Why have real wages fallen so much?

We can describe real wages by the following identity:

$$\frac{W}{P} \equiv \alpha \left(\frac{Y}{N}\right)\left(\frac{P_Y}{P}\right)$$

where W is the wage per worker, P is the consumer price level, a is the share of wages in value added, Y is real value added, N is the number of workers, and $P_Y$ is the price index of value added. Comparing 1992 with 1991, the key facts are that real wages fell by about 33 percent. Real GDP fell by 20 percent and employment fell by 4 percent, so that productivity fell by about 16 percent. Distinguishing the remaining two changes is more difficult. Using standard figures there is no change in the ratio of $P_Y$ to P, implying that the combined impact of changes in indirect taxes minus subsidies and in relative import prices was zero. Though this is somewhat surprising, the remaining fall in real wages must be due, at least partly, to a fall in $\alpha$ (i.e., a rise in the profit mark-up). Though national accounts data are not accurate enough to confirm this, there is some evidence of a rise in the profit mark-up – though nothing like the scale asserted by the critics of price liberalization.

So why did productivity fall? Clearly because output fell and enterprises were unwilling to reduce employment. The fall in output was partly a continuation of the 15 percent decline during 1991, which in turn was undoubtedly caused primarily by the break-up of the command system of allocation and its only partial replacement by the market system. But the increased rate of decline during 1992 reflects in addition the reduction in demand during the first half of the year. Production was stabilized during the second half of the year because of the high rate of credit expansion – most of which simply induced inflation but a part of which maintained production. In this analysis, a further fall in real wages is almost inevitable as the government continues its financial squeeze in accordance with its agreement with the Central Bank.

### *Wage distribution*

What about the distribution of wages? They have become more unequal. We have not been able to obtain recent data on the inter-personal distribution of wages, but data on average wage levels across industries highlights the profound changes at work.[14] The distribution of wages across 37 different sectors of manufacturing has become increasingly unequal. This is shown in Table 9.12, which depicts the rise in the standard deviation of log wages across industries. The increase in inequality is particularly striking during the course of 1991 (0.14 to 0.41).

**Table 9.12** Wage inequality across manufacturing industries, 1991 and 1992

| | Standard deviation of $\log(w_i)$ |
|---|---|
| January–February 1991 | 0.14 |
| December 1991 | 0.41 |
| January–February 1992 | 0.46 |
| December 1992 | 0.38 |

This increase in the dispersion of wages across industries is reflected in Figure 9.2, which shows that industries which paid relatively high wages in the beginning of 1991 also tended to experience relatively rapid wage growth during 1991 and 1992. In very rough terms, approximately one-half of the final wage dispersion is an amplified version of the original wage distribution and the other half is an additional random factor.[15] The impact of both factors can be seen in Annex 4, in which industries are listed according to their initial wage level in January–February

1991. Many of the high-wage industries, such as energy and metals production, experienced very high subsequent wage growth. But, in addition, there were some unsystematic changes, with rapid wage growth occurring in some formerly low wage industries, like oil refining.

Why did wages grow more quickly in some industries than in others? One powerful explanation for the growth rate of wages across industries is the growth rate of employment across industries. This is a type of "Phillips Curve" relationship, in which relatively tight labour markets generate higher wages than slack markets.

Figure 9.3 presents a regression of the growth rate of wages against the growth rate of employment across industries, and provides strong evidence corroborating the Phillips Curve relationship. If we think of the initial level of employment as a full-employment benchmark, the change in employment then measures the level of labour market tightness in the final period. Similarly, if we think of the initial wage as incorporating all relevant industry characteristics, the change in the wage level then reflects the adjusted level of wages in the final situation. The regression then shows that a 1 percent increase in the employment rate raises wages by 2.4 percent – a magnitude similar to that in West European countries.

Finally, in order to fully understand the increase in wage inequality, we must understand why those industries with relatively high wages in 1991 were the ones which have expanded employment relatively rapidly since then. This may be an accident of history, with the industries having the least pleasant working conditions (or requiring the most skills and training) also having the best opportunities for employment growth due to expanded access to world markets.

We now take a wider view of the whole wage structure (see Table 9.13). The central policy issue has been the level of wages in the budgetary sphere, especially education and health. In the early part of the reform these wages, already below average, fell further. This, more than any other factor, contributed to a widening in the dispersion of wages across branches. (At the same time, wages in transportation as well as in finance and insurance rose sharply.) In autumn 1992, however, a new system was introduced whereby budgetary wages were systematized and indexed quarterly to the consumer price index.[16] By early 1993, there were signs that inequality from this source had been somewhat reduced.

Wages in the budgetary sphere will inevitably remain an issue. However, the new arrangement guarantees that real wages will not fall in the budgetary sector at a time when real wages and employment are likely to be falling elsewhere.[17] The

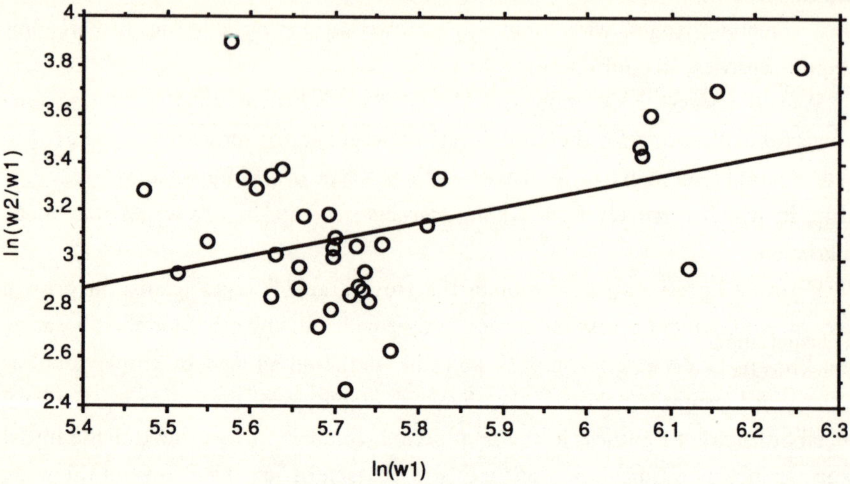


**Figure 9.2** Initial wage level and subsequent wage growth in 37 manufacturing industries
*Note*: w1=average wage in January-February 1991; w2=average wage in December 1992; ln(w2/w1)=0.678 ln(w1)-0.78; $R^2$=0.16

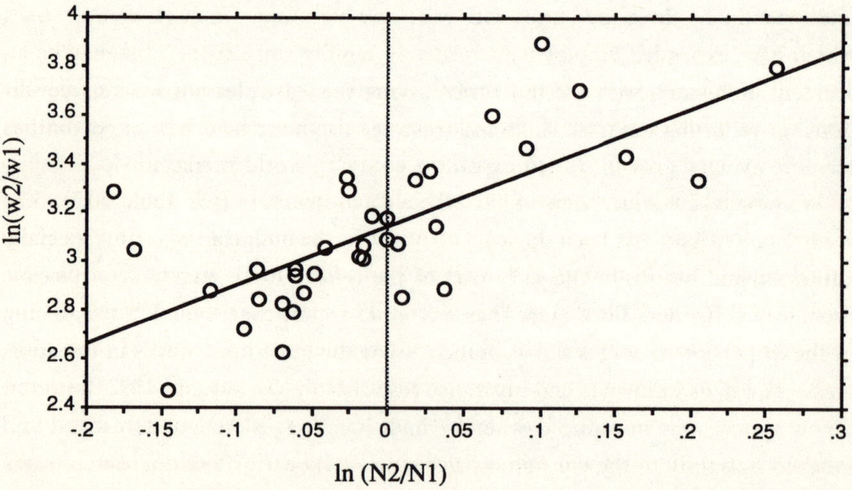


**Figure 9.3** Wage growth and employment growth across manufacturing industries, 1991 and 1992
*Note*: N2=average employment in December 1992; N1=average employment in January-February 1991; w2=average wage in December 1992; w1=average wage in January-February 1991; ln(w2/w1)=2.41 ln(N2/N1)+3.14; $R^2$=0.521

budgetary sector should not therefore experience any increasing difficulty in retaining labour.

**Table 9.13** Wage differentials across branches (as a proportion of the average wage)

| | Q1 1991 | Q4 1992 | Jan–Feb 1993 |
|---|---|---|---|
| Industry | 1.08 | 1.16 | 1.19 |
| Education | 0.81 | 0.61 | 0.82 |
| Health | 0.76 | 0.61 | 0.75 |
| Agriculture | 0.81 | 0.77 | |
| Transportation | 1.15 | 1.40 | |
| Construction | 1.25 | 1.30 | 1.26 |
| Finance and insurance | 1.51 | 2.34 | |
| Culture and art | 0.75 | 0.49 | 0.70 |
| Science | 1.23 | 0.73 | 0.68 |
| Coefficient of variation of wages across branches (%) | 0.16 | 0.28 | |

*Pensions*

The fall in real wages is a major reason for reduced real incomes in Russia, but what about transfer payments, especially pensions and child support? Russia has a well-developed pension system. Each person receives his or her individual minimum pension plus an earnings-related supplement (in early 1993 about 60 percent of pensioners received such a supplement). The minimum pension for an individual equals "the Minimum Pension" plus an additional 1 percent for each year worked in excess of 25 (men) or 20 (women). The maximum such increase to "the Minimum Pension" is 20 percent. Since most women work for most of their adult lives, the minimum pension for most people is 20 percent above "the Minimum Pension". Only about 100,000 old people get less than "the Minimum Pension".

Details on minimum and average pensions are given in Table 9.1 and Annex 1, which shows that the average pension is now about one and a half times 120 percent of "the Minimum Pension". This is roughly the same as in the 1980s. But the real value of the average pension has dropped substantially. In 1992 it averaged one-third of its 1991 level (though it was improving throughout the year). The pension in 1991, however, was exceptionally high by historical standards, and the real value of the average pension in 1992 was down by only about 40 percent relative to its 1985 level. In the first quarter of 1993, the individual minimum pension for the 60 percent of pensioners for whom the pension was the only source of income equaled 25 percent of the average net wage (this compares, for example, with 29 percent for the United Kingdom in 1991).[18]

How has the fall in the real pension affected the degree of inequality? It has certainly increased inequality as measured by income per head. For, even in 1991, the average monthly pension was less than the average income per head (R 266 compared with R 407). Even though some 20 percent of pensioners also have jobs, it is likely that the average pensioner lives in a household with below average income per head. Therefore, the sharp decline in the pension relative to average income helps to explain the increase in inequality of per capita income shown in Table 9.7.

The policy implications of these developments are, however, somewhat ambiguous. For, as Table 9.11 showed, pensioners are no more likely to be poor than the population at large (after taking account of different subsistence requirements). Rather, the most severe poverty problems are associated with large families.

**Table 9.14** The minimum wage

| | | Real minimum wage (1985=100) | Minimum wage as % of average wage |
|---|---|---|---|
| 1985 | | 100 | 35 |
| 1990 | | 87 | 24 |
| 1991 | | 83 | 25 |
| 1992 | | 32 | 15 |
| 1992 | Q1 | 35 | 17 |
| | Q2 | 37 | 18 |
| | Q3 | 34 | 14 |
| | Q4 | 20 | 8 |
| 1993 | Q1 | 26 | 12 |

The pension is now indexed quarterly to the CPI. This means that under high inflation, the real pension falls substantially in between upratings. But once inflation has been controlled, the average real pension (taken over a quarter) will rise by almost 15 percent. There seems no obvious need for any further steps to boost pensions, except for special local assistance to needy individuals.

In the longer term, there is a strong case for raising the pension age to the more reasonable level of 65. This could be done by raising, each year, the retirement age by half a year. Without some such step, the dependency ratio will become undesirably large.[19]

*Child benefits*

This brings us to the problem of children. Despite a fairly extensive system of child benefits, costing roughly 3 percent of GDP, child poverty is a serious problem – especially in large families and families headed by single mothers.

Benefits in April 1993 were as follows:

| | Ages 0–1.5 | Ages 1.5–6 | Ages 6–16 | Additional payment for child of single mother |
|---|---|---|---|---|
| R per month | 2,375 | 1,900 | 950 | 2,137 |
| % of av. wage | 7.7 | 6.2 | 3.1 | 7.0 |

There are also clothes allowances, adding something like 10 percent to these benefits.

The value of children's benefits is loosely tied to the minimum wage, though occasionally child benefits have been raised when the minimum wage has not. One reason why inequality has risen in Russia is therefore the fact that the minimum wage (and with it child allowances) has not risen as fast as the average wage (see Table 9.14).

Child benefits, though expensive, often fail to prevent poverty because they are non-targeted. What is needed is a larger benefit for poor families with the benefit declining to zero for richer families. Even if the means-testing is not precise, it is clearly necessary.

## 3 Unemployment: tomorrow's problem

*The unemployment rate*

Families affected by unemployment are among the poorest in Russia. Unemployment is still relatively low but it will inevitably rise. We begin by discussing the current situation and end with some remarks about the future.

The official statistics of unemployment are based on employment office data. Those recorded as "out of employment" are registered job-seekers who are out of work and available for work. This definition approximates the OECD/ILO definitions of unemployment, but it excludes job-seekers who do not use the employment exchanges.

In February 1993, 1.5 percent of the labour force was "out of employment". At the same time, only 0.6 percent of the labour force received unemployment benefits. This is because laid-off workers continue to be paid during the first three months of unemployment by their former employer,[20] and because benefit recipients cannot refuse reasonable job offers.

Since only about one-third of vacancies are registered at the job centers, many unemployed workers would not register if it were not a condition for receiving benefits.[21] But even the benefit requirement is not sufficient to ensure that all unemployed people register. The World Bank/Goskomstat household survey shows an unemployment rate of 3 percent.

In this survey, the unemployment rates are roughly the same for both men and women. But among the "registered unemployed" (a category in between "out of employment" and "benefit-recipients"), three-quarters are female. An unemployment rate of 3 percent is low by international standards, though we should note that an additional 9 percent of the industrial labour force was estimated in December 1992 to be working reduced hours (often involuntarily).

### *Income while unemployed*

Laid-off workers receive the following percentage of their previous nominal wage:

| *Period* | *Percentage* |
|---|---|
| First three months | 100 (from employer) |
| Next three months | 75 (benefit) |
| four months | 60 (benefit) |
| five months | 45 (benefit) |

The minimum benefit is equal to the minimum wage, which is indexed quarterly to the consumer price index and in spring 1993 was about 14 percent of the average wage.[22] In addition, all new labour force entrants who are unemployed get the minimum wage. In a period of high inflation, the minimum becomes binding for the vast majority of unemployed people – which is why the average unemployment benefit payment has typically been close to the minimum wage.[23]

If inflation continues at its current rate and unemployment rises, unemployment benefits will surely become an issue, and the real value of the minimum benefit may have to be raised. A better policy would be to control inflation.

### *Employment policy*

The future of employment will become a central social and economic issue in the reform. One argument against lay-offs is that enterprises provide many crucial social services to their employees. The typical Russian enterprise spends 35–40 percent of its wage bill on social services. But some of this, such as housing, would undoubtedly continue to be provided even after workers are disemployed. A transfer of responsibility for social benefits to the oblasts is urgent, but this should not be allowed to impede the adjustment process. A constructive framework for employment policies would have the following elements:

1. Unproductive workers should not be retained when output contracts. To contain inflation, unemployment must rise toward West European levels. In this process, it is important to ensure the maximum productivity for any particular level of employment. Thus employment must decline with output. In Russia, manufacturing output fell by 20 percent in 1992 and employment only fell by 4 percent. In the future, when output contracts, workers must be released for more productive employment in new spheres of activity.
2. Unemployed workers should be offered all possible help in becoming employable in new fields. A major national program of training is needed for unemployed people as well as for workers. Most of this training should focus on commercial skills, which are still relatively scarce in Russia. The training should be of a quality appropriate for the high educational level of the unemployed.[24]
3. Unemployment benefits should continue to be payable only for a limited duration. Beyond that time, income maintenance should be conditional on participation in training or public works programs. If this is not done, West European experience suggests that it will be impossible to prevent the build-up of long-term unemployment, which demoralizes the unemployed and does little to contain inflation. The proposed Restructuring Fund should expect to devote substantial resources to training and works programs, organized in conjunction

with the oblasts. Many of these capacities cannot be developed effectively through the enterprises themselves.

4. In company towns, a different approach is needed, since the local enterprises will have to be helped to sustain their employment. But this should be the exception, not the rule.

## 4 Regional differences

A major new source of inequality in Russia will be regional differences in income and employment. Under communism, inequality between regions was mitigated by the administrative transfer of resources from the rich to the poor regions. But during the reform, such automatic transfers had to be reduced in order to cut public expenditure and to increase incentives. This has already altered the distribution of real income between regions.

We look first at the simple inequality of money incomes across regions (Table 9.15a). For a long time, the Far East and the North had the highest incomes, while the North Caucasus, Central Chernozem, and Volgo-Vyatka were the poorest. But since the first month of the reform (January 1992), incomes have grown well above average in the North and the Far East, as well as in Siberia – areas rich in natural resources. At the same time, money incomes have grown much more slowly in the Central region (which includes Moscow) and the North West (which includes St Petersburg), due to the loss of privileges associated with the old administrative system.

However, before any firm conclusions can be drawn, we need to allow for differential inflation across the regions. Data only exist for food prices; these are shown in Table 9.15b. The highest prices are in the Far East, North, North West, and Central regions. The lowest are in North Caucasus, Central Chernozem, and the Povolozhsky. There is thus some positive correlation between the levels of prices and incomes (0.5).

There is also a positive correlation (0.5) between the change in prices and incomes, but even so there is some change in the distribution of real income. In Table 9.15c, we show comparative levels of real income obtained by dividing money income by food prices. This shows that most of the areas which had real incomes above the national average also experienced higher than average growth rates. The striking exception is the Central region.

As Table 9.16 shows, the purchasing power of ruble incomes has declined sharply in the North West and Central regions since the first month of the reform (we should note, however, that we have no data on hard currency earnings). In most other regions, the so-called "provinces," real income has risen— especially in Siberia and the Urals. The slowest growth has occurred in the Volga-Vyatka region which had a highly militarized economy.

Clearly these changes are primarily the result of economic forces, which will operate with increasing force. It seems unlikely that the political process will undertake sufficient redistribution to offset them.

Interestingly, with the exception of the North, unemployment rates are also highest in those areas where incomes have risen least – the North West, Central, and Volga-Vyatka regions (see Table 9.17). The correlation is 0.43. Thus there is a kind of regional Phillips Curve.

**Table 9.15 a** Regional income differences: nominal income per capita (as percentage of average)

| | Jan 92 | Apr 92 | Jul 92 | Oct 92 | Jan 93 | Mar 93 |
|---|---|---|---|---|---|---|
| Russia | 100.0 | 100.0 | 100.0 | 100.0 | 100.0 | 100.0 |
| North | 117.3 | 137.2 | 129.1 | 127.4 | 137.3 | 146.3 |
| North-west | 111.6 | 88.5 | 73.2 | 74.8 | 72.3 | 75.1 |
| Central | 118.5 | 112.0 | 94.4 | 98.8 | 90.0 | 85.3 |
| Volgo-Vyatka | 84.7 | 80.9 | 82.5 | 76.2 | 79.6 | 76.4 |
| Central-Chernozem | 80.3 | 71.4 | 69.3 | 81.9 | 79.5 | 76.0 |
| Povolzhsky | 89.3 | 88.5 | 82.7 | 92.1 | 98.4 | 91.4 |
| North Caucasus | 68.5 | 61.7 | 57.2 | 73.1 | 65.9 | 75.1 |
| Urals | 97.0 | 89.3 | 104.1 | 99.6 | 102.0 | 101.7 |
| West Siberia | 103.7 | 127.9 | 138.4 | 130.8 | 142.4 | 144.6 |
| East Siberia | 103.8 | 124.5 | 125.2 | 117.4 | 119.0 | 120.7 |
| Far East | 124.6 | 139.5 | 193.1 | 152.2 | 150.4 | 155.4 |
| Average CR/month | 783 | 1872 | 3553 | 5240 | 8269 | 14470 |
| Coefficient of variation | 0.18 | 0.27 | 0.38 | 0.26 | 0.29 | 0.30 |

**Table 9.15 b** Regional income differences: food price index (as percentage of average)

| | Jan 92 | Apr 92 | Jul 92 | Oct 92 | Jan 93 | Mar 93 |
|---|---|---|---|---|---|---|
| Russia | 100.0 | 100.0 | 100.0 | 100.0 | 100.0 | 100.0 |
| North | 91.1 | 116.4 | 108.2 | 119.5 | 110.6 | 114.2 |
| North-west | 123.2 | 120.2 | 113.4 | 102.7 | 101.6 | 117.4 |
| Central | 107.1 | 94.5 | 105.0 | 105.7 | 117.9 | 112.9 |
| Volgo-Vyatka | 95.0 | 98.0 | 94.5 | 86.8 | 87.2 | 91.3 |
| Central-Chernozem | 95.0 | 76.7 | 78.8 | 81.5 | 74.1 | 75.3 |
| Povolzhsky | 82.9 | 79.6 | 78.8 | 78.5 | 71.6 | 72.4 |
| North Caucasus | 92.3 | 89.6 | 82.5 | 89.4 | 87.6 | 87.3 |
| Urals | 99.0 | 102.0 | 104.7 | 107.8 | 94.1 | 90.1 |
| West Siberia | 84.5 | 106.3 | 93.0 | 95.8 | 96.4 | 92.9 |
| East Siberia | 97.3 | 121.8 | 107.4 | 95.5 | 102.6 | 100.2 |
| Far East | 110.7 | 123.9 | 134.1 | 144.7 | 138.1 | 137.6 |
| Coefficient of variation | 0.12 | 0.16 | 0.17 | 0.19 | 0.20 | 0.20 |

**Table 9.15 c** Regional income differences: real per capita income (money income/food price index) (as percentage of average)

| | Jan 92 | Apr 92 | Jul 92 | Oct 92 | Jan 93 | Mar 93 |
|---|---|---|---|---|---|---|
| Russia | 100.0 | 100.0 | 100.0 | 100.0 | 100.0 | 100.0 |
| North | 128.8 | 117.9 | 119.3 | 106.6 | 124.1 | 128.1 |
| North-west | 90.6 | 73.6 | 64.6 | 72.8 | 71.2 | 64.0 |
| Central | 110.6 | 118.5 | 89.9 | 93.5 | 76.3 | 75.6 |
| Volgo-Vyatka | 89.2 | 82.6 | 87.3 | 87.8 | 91.3 | 83.7 |
| Central-Chernozem | 84.5 | 93.1 | 87.9 | 100.5 | 107.3 | 100.9 |
| Povolzhsky | 107.7 | 111.2 | 104.9 | 117.3 | 137.4 | 126.2 |
| North Caucasus | 74.2 | 68.9 | 69.3 | 81.8 | 75.2 | 86.0 |
| Urals | 98.0 | 87.5 | 99.4 | 92.4 | 108.4 | 112.9 |
| West Siberia | 112.7 | 120.3 | 148.8 | 136.5 | 147.7 | 155.7 |
| East Siberia | 106.7 | 102.2 | 116.6 | 122.9 | 116.0 | 120.5 |
| Far East | 112.6 | 112.6 | 144.0 | 105.2 | 108.9 | 112.9 |
| Coefficient of variation | 0.16 | 0.19 | 0.27 | 0.18 | 0.24 | 0.25 |

**Table 9.16** Changes in income, food prices, and real income, January 1992-March 1993 (Jan 1992=1.0)

| | Nominal income per capita | Food prices | Real income per capita |
|---|---|---|---|
| Russia | 18.49 | 15.31 | 1.21 |
| North | 23.05 | 19.20 | 1.20 |
| North-west | 12.44 | 14.60 | 0.85 |
| Central | 13.31 | 16.15 | 0.83 |
| Volgo-Vyatka | 16.66 | 14.71 | 1.13 |
| Central-Chernozem | 17.50 | 12.13 | 1.44 |
| Povolzhsky | 18.93 | 13.36 | 1.42 |
| North Caucasus | 20.52 | 14.49 | 1.42 |
| Urals | 19.38 | 13.92 | 1.39 |
| West Siberia | 25.78 | 16.83 | 1.53 |
| East Siberia | 21.49 | 15.76 | 1.36 |
| Far East | 23.05 | 19.03 | 1.21 |
| Coefficient of variation | 0.21 | 0.14 | 0.19 |

**Table 9.17** Out of employment by region, February 1993

| | 'Out of employment' (thousands) | Unemployment rate (percent) |
|---|---|---|
| North | 78.2 | 2.6 |
| North-west | 84.7 | 2.1 |
| Central | 235.3 | 1.6 |
| Volgo-Vyatka | 88.4 | 2.1 |
| Central-Chernozem | 42.4 | 1.1 |
| Povolzhsky | 96.9 | 1.2 |
| North Caucasus | 95.2 | 1.2 |
| Urals | 134.1 | 1.3 |
| West Siberia | 103.1 | 1.4 |
| Eastern Siberia | 50.1 | 1.1 |
| Far East | 53.6 | 1.4 |

## Conclusion

We draw seven main conclusions about the record to date:

1. Average consumption (properly measured) fell in 1992 to perhaps 80 percent of its 1991 level. At the same time, the reduction of queuing has been a major welfare gain. The fall in consumption is due primarily to the ongoing fall in output caused by the breakdown of the old command system.
2. Food consumption has fallen little; the main falls in consumption have been in other goods and in services. Relative food prices have been kept low by subsidies and credits to the agricultural sector.
3. Inequality has risen, especially at the bottom end of the income distribution. Measured real income at the lower decile in March–April 1993 was only one-third of its level in 1991 and consumption at that level may have fallen by one-half.
4. The rise in inequality is mainly due to a rise in wage dispersion and the fall in the ratio of children's benefits to the average wage.
5. The incidence of poverty is highest in large families and families headed by single parents, while the distribution of well-being among pensioners is similar to the population at large.
6. The families of the unemployed, though small in number, are also highly prone to poverty. This is largely due to the effect of inflation in eroding the value of earnings-related benefits.
7. Regional inequality has risen due to the impact of economic forces and diminished political will for redistributive programs.

Looking to the future, there are 4 main points:

1. Financial stabilization will inevitably lead to further temporary falls in output and living standards.
2. Wage dispersion will continue to widen, aggravating the poverty problem.
3. The main problem with the social safety net is children's benefits, which should be increased in real terms for poor families and reduced for others by means-testing. Some savings on pensions would be possible if the retirement age is gradually raised.
4. Unemployment is bound to rise. The effects of this secular rise could be extremely serious unless major training programs are implemented, especially in market-orientated skills.

Before the reform began, many observers forecast a social catastrophe. It has not occurred, though there are major problems— many of which will get worse. But Russia has the means to overcome them.

Annex 1 Wages, incomes, and pensions

| | Income (R bn) | Consumers' Expenditure (R bn) | Average wage (R per month) | Average pension (R per month) | Minimun pension (R per month) |
|---|---|---|---|---|---|
| 1985 | 245 | 202 | 201 | 75 | 50 |
| 1986 | 254 | 207 | 207 | 77 | 50 |
| 1987 | 264 | 213 | 216 | 80 | 60 |
| 1988 | 287 | 228 | 235 | 83 | 60 |
| 1989 | 325 | 250 | 259 | 87 | 60 |
| 1990 | 385 | 290 | 297 | 102 | 70 |
| 1991 | 733 | 510 | 516 | 266 | 161 |
| 1992 | 6,243 | 3,772 | 6,011 | 1,667 | 1,102 |
| 1992 | | | | | |
| January | 119 | | 1,438 | 438 | 342 |
| February | 174 | | 2,004 | 638 | 542 |
| March | 226 | | 2,726 | 638 | 542 |
| April | 276 | | 3,024 | 738 | 642 |
| May | 274 | | 3,672 | 1,383 | 900 |
| June | 369 | | 5,067 | 1,383 | 900 |
| July | 511 | 259 | 5,452 | 1,383 | 900 |
| August | 539 | 305 | 5,870 | 1,803 | 1,320 |
| September | 624 | 386 | 7,379 | 1,803 | 1,320 |
| October | 758 | 469 | 8,853 | 1,803 | 1,320 |
| November | 907 | 558 | 10,576 | 4,000 | 2,250 |
| December | 1,466 | 851 | 16,071 | 4,000 | 2,250 |

**Annex 2** Per capita income distribution, April 1993

| R/month | Percentage of the population | Cumulative percentage |
|---|---|---|
| <3000 | 2.0 | 2.0 |
| 3001–4000 | 3.8 | 5.8 |
| 4001–5000 | 5.7 | 11.5 |
| 5001–6000 | 7.1 | 18.6 |
| 6001–7000 | 7.8 | 26.4 |
| 7001–8000 | 7.9 | 34.3 |
| 8001–9000 | 7.7 | 42.0 |
| 9001–10000 | 7.3 | 49.3 |
| 10001–11000 | 6.7 | 56.0 |
| 11001–12000 | 6.1 | 62.1 |
| 12001–13000 | 5.5 | 67.6 |
| 13001–14000 | 4.9 | 72.5 |
| 14001–15000 | 4.3 | 76.8 |
| 15001–16000 | 3.8 | 80.6 |
| 16001–17000 | 3.4 | 84.0 |
| 17001–18000 | 2.9 | 86.9 |
| 18001–19000 | 2.6 | 89.5 |
| 19001–20000 | 2.3 | 91.8 |
| >20000 | 8.2 | 100.0 |

**Annex 3** Income distributions relative to poverty level, Q3 1992 (income as % of relevant poverty level)

| | <50% | 51–100% | 101–150% | 151–200% | >200% |
|---|---|---|---|---|---|
| Total population | 11 | 26 | 25 | 15 | 23 |
| Children ages 0–6 | 16 | 30 | 22 | 13 | 19 |
| Children ages 7–15 | 16 | 31 | 25 | 12 | 17 |
| Young adults ages 16–30 | 13 | 23 | 23 | 15 | 26 |
| Women ages 31–54 | 10 | 25 | 25 | 15 | 25 |
| Men ages 31–59 | 9 | 25 | 25 | 15 | 25 |
| Women older than 55 | 5 | 29 | 26 | 17 | 23 |
| Men older than 60 | 3 | 19 | 29 | 19 | 30 |

**Annex 4** Wages, wage growth, and employment growth across manufacturing industries

| | Wage (R/month) Jan–Feb 1991 | Dec 92 wage/ Jan–Feb 91 wage (minus mean) | Employment growth (%) Jan–Feb 91 to Dec 92 (minus mean growth) |
|---|---|---|---|
| Gas | 520 | 21.0 | 29.7 |
| Oil extraction | 470 | 16.6 | 14.0 |
| Fish | 455 | -4.4 | -5.7 |
| Coal | 435 | 12.7 | 7.5 |
| Electricity | 430 | 6.9 | 17.3 |
| Non-ferrous metals | 430 | 8.1 | 9.8 |
| Ferrous metals | 338 | 4.3 | 2.1 |
| Cellulose | 333 | -0.7 | 3.6 |
| Other machinery | 320 | -10.0 | -7.2 |
| Automobile production | 317 | -2.4 | -1.1 |
| Electrical engineering | 312 | -7.0 | -6.4 |
| Transport equipment | 310 | -4.7 | -3.3 |
| Chemical and petrochemical machinery | 309 | -6.2 | -4.8 |
| Textiles | 308 | -5.8 | 4.1 |
| Timber | 307 | -2.7 | -3.7 |
| Machinery for light and food industries | 304 | -6.5 | 1.3 |
| Instrument making | 303 | -12.0 | -13.0 |
| Building materials construction | 299 | -1.9 | 0.3 |
| Medical equipment | 299 | -2.8 | -15.2 |
| Wood processing | 298 | -3.5 | -1.1 |
| Polygrahpic industry | 297 | -7.5 | -5.7 |
| Chemicals | 297 | 0.3 | -0.6 |
| Machine-tool construction | 293 | -8.7 | -8.7 |
| Microbiology production | 288 | 0.2 | 0.0 |
| Metallurgical machinery | 286 | -4.4 | -7.5 |
| Tractor and agricultural machinery | 286 | -6.0 | -10.6 |
| Flour and mixed fodder | 281 | 5.1 | 3.3 |
| Leather, boot and shoe industry | 279 | -3.4 | -1.4 |
| Others | 277 | -6.7 | -7.9 |
| Petrochemicals | 277 | 4.4 | -2.4 |
| Meat and milk processing | 273 | 3.0 | -2.2 |
| Agricultural complex enterprises | 269 | 4.3 | 23.1 |
| Oil refining | 264 | 25.1 | 10.9 |
| Glass, porcelain and faience | 257 | -2.3 | 0.8 |
| Sewing | 248 | -5.0 | -5.4 |
| Wood-chemical | 238 | 2.7 | -13.7 |
| Mean | 320 | | |

Note: Mean (unweighted) wage change was 24 times and mean (unweighted) employment growth was 0.4 percent.

## Notes

* The views expressed in this paper are those of the authors alone, and do not necessarily represent the views of either the Russian or US Governments or any agencies thereof. The authors would like to thank Eugene Gontmacher, Timothy King, and Barry Popkin for several extremely beneficial discussions. All data are from Goskomstat (the Russian State Statistical Committee) unless otherwise noted. Further details can be obtained from *Russian Economic Trends* (see references).

1. In these statistics, household income is measured at the point of payment, so that income is the sum of *recorded* wage payments, pension payments, and so on. Of this household income, some is devoted to increased holdings of rubles (currency and deposits), some to taxes, and the remainder is recorded as consumers' expenditure. Real values of income and expenditure are then calculated by deflating the consumer price index (CPI).
2. The savings rate is defined as savings divided by disposable income (income minus direct taxes). The other difference between income and consumption is direct taxes.
3. The inflation tax paid by households (assets × inflation rate) equaled over 100% of household income in 1991 and (ignoring the January 1992 price jump) 40% of household income in 1992.
4. More precisely, the new level of utility is equal to $(1/2)\alpha$ times the old level of utility, assuming that X/2 consumption is unchanged.
5. Any loss of money income due to queuing has already been incorporated into our measure of income. Here we only include the losses due to the disutility of queuing relative to the alternative activity.
6. For example, in November 1992, the survey data indicate that expenditure per capita for families with one or more workers was R 6,455, and for families with pensioners, R 2,809.

Real measured consumers' expenditure and retail sales (1985=100)

| | Measured consumers' expenditures | Retail sales |
|---|---|---|
| 1985 | 100.0 | 100.0 |
| 1991 | 113.0 | 109.0 |
| 1992 | 48.9 | 50.3 |

*Note*: The table depicts the relevant nominal figure deflated by the Soviet Union retail price index for 1985–1990 and the Russian consumer price index for 1991 onwards.

Multiplying the worker figure by 120 million and the pensioner figure by 30 million, we obtain an estimate of aggregate consumers' expenditure of R 859 bn. In the same month, measured consumers' expenditure was R 558 bn. The legitimacy of this calculation is, however, somewhat uncertain.

Retail sales figures throw a little further light on the issue. Officially measured retail sales fell slightly less during 1992 than measured consumption (see below). Retail sales are based on data for sales of goods through standard retail outlets, whether privatized or not. They do include the vast majority of sales, including goods re-sold on the street, but exclude goods entering the retail market through the new cooperatives, "commercial shops", kolkhoz and street markets. The share of these informal sales has surely risen, implying a larger downward bias in the measured retail sales figure.

7. The elasticity of substitution between food and other goods is less than one.
8. The survey sample was originally selected from a sample of enterprises and households in the 1950s, and replacements are made as extant participants disappear.
9. Atkinson and Micklewright (1992), p.137. UK data are from the Family Expenditure Survey using "normal earnings". Russian data relate to income within the month; the full income distribution for April 1993 is given in Annex 2.
10. See Popkin, Mozhina, and Baturin (1992). The income needed for different age groups were the following proportions of the average in November 1992: children ages 0-6, 0.78; children 7-17, 1.16; adult males, 1.26; adult females, 1.05; and pensioner adults, 0.71. The share of food for each of the groups is (%): 74, 74, 62, 62, and 83.
11. One problem with this methodology is that it assumes an individual can continually spend his entire disposable income. But if individuals wish to maintain some level of real balances, the inflation tax must be subtracted from disposable income before obtaining a measure of potential consumption. For extremely poor people, this may not be a particularly important caveat.
12. The table is based on preliminary analysis of data on 5,000 families. Details are given in Annex 3, including analysis of the very poor.
13. The minimum individual pension was around R 1,300 per month in the third quarter of 1992 (after allowing for the 20 percent tenure supplement discussed below), while the subsistence requirement for older people averaged over R 1,400. It follows that pensioners can only have been below the poverty threshold if they lived in large families or if their job tenure was unusually short.
14. We do have data for the wage distribution across workers in September 1991, which yield the following statistics: lower decile/median=0.48, top decile/median=2.11. The standard deviation of log wages is 0.53. It is interesting to note that in medium-sized firms in 1991 Q3, wages across job categories were in the following ratios:

| | |
|---|---|
| Unskilled | 1.0 |
| Skilled | 2.7 |
| Professional | 2.9 |
| Vice director | 4.3 |

There was no marked change over the subsequent year in firms of all sizes except that wages of managers in large firms grew more rapidly than average. Of all firms in the sample, 25 percent reported an increased spread of wages and 17 percent a decreased spread.

15. The regression of log $w_2$ on log $w_1$ yields: log $w_2$=1.68 log $w_1$- 0.78, with a standard error of 0.29 and an $R_2$ of 0.53. Thus var(log $w_2$)=$1.68^2$var (log $w_1$)+$0.29^2$=2.82var(log $w_1$)+0.089=2.82 (.035)+0.08=0.18.
16. In April 1993, the minimum wage in the budgetary sphere was raised to R 8,125 (equal to the minimum pension). This was 34 percent of the average wage (R 23,559) at the beginning of April, but a declining proportion over the subsequent three months (since the minimum wage is uprated only once per quarter). All other budgetary wages are fixed multiples of the minimum budgetary wage.

17. If the rate of inflation falls, and indexation remains quarterly, the average real wage over the quarter will rise.
18. For the purposes of this comparison, housing costs are excluded from the incomes of pensioners and workers in the United Kingdom.
19. The share of national income spent on state pensions is slightly more than 6%; in the U.K. it is 6%.
20. The first two months' pay is essentially severance pay since it is paid whether or not the person is unemployed.
21. Income maintenance from the third month onwards requires registration during the first two weeks of unemployment.
22. The minimum wage was raised to R 4,275 per month on April 1–18 percent of the average wage.
23. The minimum wage actually exceeded the average unemployment benefit during several months in late 1992 and early 1993. There seems to have been delays in adjusting the payment of benefits to changes in the minimum wage.
24. The registered unemployed have obtained the following educational levels:

| Educational level | % of registered unemployed |
|---|---|
| Higher education | 18 |
| Specialized secondary education | 27 |
| General secondary education | 38 |
| Uncompleted secondary education | 17 |

## References

Anthony Atkinson and John Micklewright, *Economic transformation in Eastern Europe and the distribution of income*, Cambridge University Press, 1992.

Government of the Russian Federation, *Russian Economic Trends,* Whurr Publishers (Fax 913 843 1221 (US), 071 359 5979 (UK)).

Victor Polterovich, "Rationing, Queues, and Black Markets", *Econometrica*, 61:1-28.

Barry Popkin, Marina Mozhina, and Alexander Baturin, "The Development of a Subsistence Income Level in the Russian Federation", mimeo, 1992.

World Bank, *Russian Economic Reform: Crossing the Threshold of Structural Change*, 1992.

# 10 Has Poland Been Useful as a Model for Russia?*

*Anders Åslund*

## Introduction

The change of economic system in Russia has primarily been inspired by the systemic changes in Poland. Former Acting Prime Minister Yegor Gaidar and other top reformers had deep insights in the Polish reform process. Poland offered a comprehensive model, and the literature on its systemic changes is good, well-spread, and rather comprehensive (Lipton and Sachs, 1990; Balcerowicz, 1992). Most of the leading foreign advisers to the Russian government had previously assisted the Polish government.[1] At present, however, it is striking how different these two transformations have become. In many regards, Russia seems to fail where Poland succeeded and vice versa. While Poland was relatively successful in stabilization, Russia has accomplished little to date, but it has done more than Poland in privatisation. Liberalization has gone far in both places, but initially it went further in Poland than in Russia.

A large number of questions arise. Was Poland a relevant model at all? Or would it have been better to look upon, for instance, China, Japan, West Germany, South Korea, Taiwan or Singapore, as a variety of people have suggested in the debate both in Russia and the West. In what essential ways did Poland differ from Russia? What alterations in the reforms did these differences call for? Were such changes made in the reforms?

I shall devote the first section of this paper to a comparison of the preconditions in Poland and Russia, respectively. A second section will discuss why stabilization and liberalization have been relatively less successful in Russia than in Poland. The third section will address the issue of large-scale privatization, and why it appears to be more successful in Russia than in Poland. In a fourth and final section, the concluding questions will be raised: to what extent, and in what regards was Poland relevant as a model?[2]

## How different were preconditions?

A variety of preconditions may be of relevance to transforming an economic system. Critics of the reformist government in Russia, such as Oleg Bogomolov (1992), tend to emphasize three features of Poland: predominant private agriculture, the Catholic church and the Solidarity trade union, implying that both the Polish economy and society were more mature and therefore Poland has little to teach Russia. However, the arguments have not been well elaborated, and one difference is far too often presented as an insurmountable obstacle to any comparison between two countries. We need an analytical framework. In this section, prime themes will be the political preconditions, the dissolution of the Soviet Union, the amount of market economic instruments at hand, the degree of economic distortions, the financial situation, the foreign financial position, and export potential. This is a selection, but presumably it includes the most relevant preconditions.

At the outset of the Russian systemic changes at the end of 1991, the political situation was pretty different in comparison with Poland in late 1989. With regard to democratic elections, Russia had the advantage of having a democratically-elected president, while Poland still had communist General Wojciech Jaruzelski as president. Both countries had parliaments that were partially democratic. In Poland, only 35 percent of the seats in the lower house of parliament were open to free elections in June 1989, while the Russian parliamentary elections in March 1990 were rather haphazard, with a negative selection of little-known candidates and no party system. Poland was much more advanced in terms of social organisations. It made a lot of difference that Poland had the Catholic church, the Solidarity trade union, in addition to a lot of other old or new political and social organisations. Much of civil society was already in existence in Poland or had never been demolished. The freedom and diversity of the public debate was well developed in both countries, with a wide-ranging economic debate. The problem was not the degree of freedom but the low quality of much of the debate in both countries.

Still, the foremost difference between the political situation in Poland and Russia was that the old elite had been and remained much stronger in Russia. It was bigger, richer, more powerful, more convinced in its Marxist-Leninism and far more prepared to fight for its survival, as the abortive coups in August 1991 and October 1993 proved.

Another important difference was the dissolution of the Soviet Union and the emergence of a "near abroad" of former Soviet republics around Russia. On the one hand, Russia was left with a number of duties, or presumed duties, toward former Soviet republics and old Soviet institutions. There was no clear break with the former Soviet republics. Agreements had to be reached between them and Russia on the division of union property, including the military and foreign debts and assets, on currency, payments, and trade conditions, such as tariffs and prices. On the other hand, many Russian state institutions were either missing or rudimentary and had to be created. Moreover, Russia itself is a multi-ethnic state and formally a federation.

During the 1980s, Poland had established many market-oriented institutions and more than one-third of the Polish labour force worked in the private sector before the real change of economic system. In fact, Poland had some kind of market socialism. For instance, money was active and unified. A variety of private enterprises and foreign ventures had existed for a long time. In Russia, the first departure from the old system occurred when the Law on State Enterprises went into force in January 1988 and the Law on Co-operatives in May 1988 (Åslund, 1991). Russia's emerging elements of a market economy were slight in comparison with Poland. Moreover, they appeared rather distorted, for instance, with a considerable development of commercial banks and commodity exchanges, but rather little petty trade. Capitalism had been destroyed in Poland, but its memory was still alive, unlike in Russia. The longer capitalism had been dead, the less of it remained.

Similarly, the economic structure had become all the more distorted the longer communism had lasted. These distortions were of all kinds. First, the Russian economy was far more dominated by raw material extraction and the military-industrial complex. Second, "gigantomania", the predilection for large-scale firms, had developed further here than anywhere else in the world. Third, the social and physical infrastructure as well as services had been increasingly neglected over the years. Fourth, artificially long land hauls of goods back and forth over the large country prevailed. Fifth, trading patterns both with the outside world and within the country were largely politically or bureaucratically determined. Because of greater structural distortions in Russia, greater early structural changes would have been natural. However, it is not evident how macroeconomic performance would be affected. On the one hand, it could be argued that more restructuring would lead to greater disruption and thus a deeper decline. On the other hand, Russia had far greater resources available than Poland, many in the form of exportable goods.

The domestic financial situation was extremely poor in Russia, far worse than in Poland. In 1991, much of tax collection collapsed as the Soviet Union disintegrated. The tax system was not the least reformed and needed great amendments instantly. Starting in 1990, public expenditures, both various subsidies and social expenditures, had run out of control. Monetary control was even worse because of both the dissolution of the Soviet Union and the lack of prior reform. It was unclear which institution was to pursue monetary policy and in what territory it would be pursued. A multitude of technical problems complicated the situation (Sachs and Lipton, 1993).

The foreign financial standing of Russia, however, was much better than the Polish position. Even when Russia took over the servicing of the whole Soviet foreign debt, its formal debt service ratio for 1992 stopped at 62 percent ("Platezhnyi", 1993). This is what Hungary had managed at the outset of its transition to a market economy, though the debt service ratio cannot be looked upon in isolation from the domestic financial situation, which was far worse in Russia. Thus, the Russian foreign debt situation was difficult but not altogether hopeless, as it had been in Poland.

In most regards, Russia found itself in a more difficult situation than Poland, but these preconditions are difficult to assess: it is not obvious what role they are to play, or what problems may turn out to be decisive. Let us look upon what has actually happened as a way to put them into an analytical framework. In each case, I shall try to identify the crucial causes of success or failure, while trying to bring out major complications or achievements.

## Why has Russia's stabilization and liberalization been less successful than Poland's?

Let us begin by turning to the greatest complications in the Russian transformation since January 1992. The outstanding failure in the Russian change of economic system has been high inflation, reaching some 2,500 percent in 1992. Another major shortcoming has been the apparent rise of corruption and organized crime. Contrary to expectations, shortages have not been abolished, the simple explanation being that a large number of formal and informal regulations persist. The problems of capital flight and a sharply falling exchange rate may be added. It is too early to say much about the total decline in production. So far, it has been comparatively limited, and unemployment has barely started to rise in Russia, since so little stabilization has been undertaken.

The main causes behind these phenomena are easy to establish. The three sources of inflation were excessive credits from the Central Bank, huge credits to the other former Soviet republics and the budget deficit (Sachs, 1993).

The foremost shortcoming of the Central Bank was that it refused to pursue monetary policy and insisted that the money supply had to adjust to inflation rather than restraining it (Tsentralnyi, 1992). From June through October 1992, monetary expansion averaged 29 percent a month (*Russian Economic Trends*, 1993). The refinance rate stayed at 80 percent per annum, even when inflation surged to an annualised rate of 2,000 percent. The very negative interest rates provided plenty of room for bribery. In the spring of 1993, a practice had developed whereby commercial banks paid 15 percent of a three-month credit to people in or around the Central Bank in the form of bribes. Thus, the loose monetary policy did not only lead to high inflation but also to massive corruption and the enrichment of a small group of people who benefited from the low interest rates, while the rest of society was left paying the sizeable inflation tax.

This behaviour of the Central Bank can partly be explained by the failure of the reformers to gain control over it, because it was subordinate to the parliament. In Poland, there was relatively limited disagreement between the Ministry of Finance and the National Bank. Both in Poland and in Russia, the chairman of the Central Bank was an old communist technocrat during the crucial period.[3] It is difficult to generalize on the basis of two persons, but it appears characteristic that in Poland it worked to co-opt an old communist, while in Russia it did not. An alternative argument could be made that Poland's Baka was foremost an academic economist, while Gerashchenko was only a civil servant with a narrow outlook. However, the point is that there were so few intellectuals of sufficient standing in Russia who could take on major government responsibilities. A third layer of problems in the Central Bank was most apparent during the first half of 1991 under the chairmanship of Georgy Matiukhin. Then, a large number of technical problems mounted, notably the highly centralized and slow clearing of payments, contributing to large inter-enterprise arrears (Sachs and Lipton, 1993; Rostowski, 1993).

Similar problems emerged in the Ministry of Finance, even though it was under the political control of the reformers. An old Soviet Ministry of Finance technocrat, Vasily Barchuk was appointed Minister of Finance in the spring of 1992, and he was neither intellectually nor psychologically prepared to play the role of a capitalist Minister of Finance, which was a contributing factor in the disintegration of macroeconomic policy in the third quarter of 1992 (though the major cause was political). The Russian Ministry of Finance had very poor control over expenditures. Various lobbies were able to extract subsidies and particularly subsidised credits without the consent of the Ministry. This was true of agricultural subsidies, interest subsidies through banks, and centralized imports of mainly grain and medicine. The import subsidies constituted the biggest hole in the state finances and accounted for as much as 12.6 percent of the Russian GDP in 1992, according to the IMF. This was both a question of political and technical control. Typically, various authorities refused to report to each other. Thus, the Ministry of Finance could not obtain information about the finances of the pension funds within reasonable time and always had problems receiving information from the Central Bank.

The third big hole in the state finances of Russia was credits to other former Soviet republics in the ruble zone. They amounted to some 10 percent of Russia's GDP in 1992. Since they were given at a very low interest rate, and the conditions for their repayment were not settled, they appear to be actual but unintended gifts. The obvious conclusion was that the ruble zone had to be broken up into independent currency zones, each with one independent central bank, while the new currencies would be convertible, facilitating trade on ordinary market terms between these former Soviet republics. Neither Poland nor any of the alternative model countries could contribute to the understanding of this question. The relevant experience here was the break-up of the Habsburg Empire, when Czechoslovakia was first to undertake a currency reform and pursued the most conservative economic policy. It also turned out to be the only economically successful country in the region and survived as a democracy until the Nazi troops took over (Pasvolsky, 1928; Sargent, 1986). The Baltic states of Estonia and Latvia had absorbed this lesson and carried out the necessary currency reforms in the summer of 1992 (Hansson, 1993ab). Within the Russian government, the "nationalization" of the Russian ruble had been discussed since August 1991. The idea was to take control over the ruble and in effect exclude the other former Soviet republics from the ruble zone, in order to impose monetary discipline under one single monetary authority.

Unfortunately, this did not take place for a large number of reasons. Internally, Russian industrialists preferred to continue "selling" to the other former Soviet republics, being paid not by these enterprises but by their own government. A flawed argument emerged that this trade would collapse, if the ruble zone ceased.

Instead, the argument should run that since real payments had ceased, deliveries should be stopped as well. In fact, these industrialists demanded government subsidies for continuing to produce what nobody was prepared to pay for, thus harmfully delaying restructuring. For political reasons, a number of Russian politicians with nostalgia for the old empire wanted to maintain the ruble zone, in order to make it feasible to re-establish the USSR. Leaders of other republics tended to focus more upon what subsidies they could gain from Russia than on their own stabilization. A number of Western academics argued in favour of some kind of payments union (Gros, 1992; Hawrylyshyn and Williamson, 1991), but neither trust nor legal instruments were sufficient for any clearing mechanism. Any attempt at a clearing arrangement resulted in an accumulation of unpaid bills. Some drew a faulty analogy with the intended European Monetary Union, stating that it would be wrong to break up an existing monetary union, while Europe was trying to create one.

The IMF long opposed currency reforms for three reasons. It wanted a new currency to be connected with success, and hoped for a bottoming out first. What it had not realized was that the longer no proper currency functioned in a country, the deeper the fall would be, and the later the bottom would be reached. A better argument was that the technical preparations were lacking, and that a failed currency reform would have serious repercussions. A final argument, however faulty, was that Russia was relatively well off in terms of export earnings and international financing, and that it would be more difficult to raise funding for other former Soviet republics with the exception of the Baltic states. Therefore, Russia could continue subsidizing the others with cheap credits and raw materials.

Thus, a broad coalition of varied parties with bad arguments stalled the necessary separation of currencies. Finally, a currency reform required political courage from all parties concerned, and that courage was not mobilized (cf Lipton and Sachs, 1992; Dabrowski, 1993b; Åslund, 1993). The causes were a combination of intellectual shortcomings, vested interests of Russian industrialists and most former Soviet republics, and political resistance.

Russian price liberalization was formally quite wide-ranging, but a few commodities, notably energy, remained subject to price regulation. This had been the case in countries where negative effects had been apparent but manageable, such as Poland and Czechoslovakia. In Russia, however, the effects were extraordinarily harmful. Low regulated energy prices and remaining foreign trade regulations were closely interconnected. Low domestic prices of major export commodities necessitated some kind of restrictions on exports. Otherwise, exporters with access to commodities that were subject to price regulation domestically would reap enormous profits on the world market. However, Russia entered into a vicious circle. Since inflation was not under control, the fixed energy prices became ever lower in relation to the world market prices, as the exchange rate fell with inflation. For instance, in May 1993, the domestic prices of gas and coal amounted to a mere 4 percent of the world price. The low energy prices, in turn, led to huge subsidies to the coal industry, destined to exceed two percent of GDP in 1993. Even more important, the government lost at least 5 percent of GDP in budget revenue, that could easily have been raised through various taxes on energy. Thus, a liberalization of the energy price could have solved many of the problems concerning the balancing of the budget.

The export regulations included export licences, export quotas, export tariffs, compulsory exchanging of currency revenues, and initially special surrender exchange rates. The main beneficiaries of this policy were the traders involved in subsidized foreign trade, that is, exporters of oil and metals and importers of grain. Also here, massive corruption evolved. A low estimate by government experts of the amount of bribery is $0.5 bn, of which imports accounted for about one-fifth and exports for the rest. The combination of a multitude of export regulations and large-scale corruption prompted massive capital flight, assessed at $5–17 bn, depending on the definition used ("Platezhnyi", 1992).

Any shortcoming in the comprehensiveness of the reform, such as insufficient liberalization, appears to have been far more costly in Russia than in Poland. The effects of remaining price regulations were much milder in Poland. Export regulations did not exist in Poland and were quite indefensible in Russia. They were a result of domestic price regulations, and the strong vested interests of both export producers and primarily a variety of foreign trade organizations. They reflected the political strength of an old rent-seeking elite in Russia. Their power was reinforced by the greater export potential in Russia, the larger size of this old elite, and the confusion over links with the former Soviet republics.

In comparison with Poland, there was an astounding array of remnants of the old communist economic system in Russia. As late as April 1993, 2,600 industrial enterprises that had suffered from work stoppages during that month, blamed 47 percent of lost time on shortages of inputs, which is the characteristic problem of a command economy, while only 42 percent of lost time was caused by a lack of demand, which is the typical concern in a market economy.[4] The causes of persistent shortages were the large numbers of remaining regulations, but even more the behaviour of different government authorities, both at the central level and probably much more so at the regional level. The problem is that the old regulatory apparatus remained in place. If it managed, it passed new restrictive decrees. Otherwise, it just behaved as if a number of abolished regulations still existed.

The role of the West, finally, was not particularly encouraging. First, the West appeared not to have noticed President Boris Yeltsin's declaration of radical economic reform on 28 October 1991 (Yeltsin, 1991). Western eyes lingered on Soviet President Mikhail Gorbachev. Even after the Soviet Union had ceased to exist, it took some time before the West realized that Russia and its reform program were for real. Indeed, it took so much time that Western collaboration did not take place until it was too late. An ill-defined package of $24 bn was promised on 1 April 1992, but it did not lead to concrete interaction on the Russian reform program before the stabilization was undone by domestic political pressures. In the spring of 1993, however, the West managed to come up with a swift, appropriate and balanced response.

Yet, several issues turned out to be easier in Russia than in Poland. The wage pressure was limited in Russia because of a lack of credible trade unions and other social organizations. Similarly, Russia experienced surprisingly little popular pressure in favour of higher social expenditures. The problem was rather enterprise lobbies demanding subsidies. While tax collection had collapsed rather seriously in 1991, the government managed to collect about 53 percent of GDP in taxes in 1992 with surprising ease. For an administrative task like this the old Soviet apparatus functioned reasonably effectively, though presumably at the expense of legality.

The simple conclusion that comes out of this reasoning is that both liberalization and stabilization were more poorly undertaken and executed in Russia than in Poland (cf Dabrowski, 1993a; Åslund, 1993a). The Russian reform program was less comprehensive than the Polish one, and there was not the same clear sense of one package being introduced. Initially, Russia lacked proper export liberalization, a pegged exchange rate, incomes policy and foreign reserves. Still, given the complete shortage of goods and the drastic fall of output in late 1991, it appears to have been right to go ahead.

Although Russia presumably could have done better, for instance, liberalizing energy prices at the outset, it is more striking how limited the possibilities appeared in late 1991. Much of the period of what Leszek Balcerowicz (1992) calls 'extraordinary politics', or a window of opportunity, was missed. Moreover, the political underpinnings of the reform government were largely absent. Far too much of the old regulatory apparatus remained in place, notably the old State Planning Committee (simply renamed the Ministry of the Economy) and the State Price Committee. While it had been dubious to co-opt old communist top officials in Poland, it turned out to be largely harmful in Russia.

The outstanding difference in comparison with Poland is that industrial lobbies were much stronger in Russia and that they remain so (Åslund, 1993a). Their interests were cheap credits, subsidies, foreign trade rents, and low energy prices (apart from the energy industry that demanded subsidies because of the low energy prices). The only means by which both the old elite and the industrial lobbies could be beaten was democratic elections to a new parliament. Since this was a small group that made more money than ever, it would be foolhardy to believe that it would have been prepared to compromise. Therefore, the Polish model of a roundtable agreement was not applicable, but direct political confrontation appeared more useful.

## Why has large-scale privatization been so successful in Russia?

Russia's inspiration for large-scale privatization came largely from Poland and Czechoslovakia (cf Frydman, et al, 1993; Major, 1993), as is evident from the writings of Deputy Prime Minister for privatization, Anatoly Chubais (Chubais and Vishnevskaya, 1993) and his advisers Maxim Boycko and Andrei Shleifer (1993) as well as from the legislation. Large-scale privatization in Poland has to a considerable extent been a failure, since a law on mass privatization was late, passed by parliament in spring 1993, when the Russian mass privatization was already well underway. By September 1993, about 4,000 large and medium-sized enterprises (with more than 200 employees) had already been put up for voucher privatization auctions. The Czechoslovak voucher privatization, however, had started about one year earlier than the Russian voucher privatization and it had gone beyond expectations.

An important initial advantage of Russia was that after 75 years of communism, restitution was not an issue. The government of both Poland and Czechoslovakia had tried to stave away from restitution but they had not altogether succeeded.

An essential early decision was to build up a large state administration of state property committees in each of the country's 89 regions. On the one hand, it took some time and effort. On the other hand, it meant there was a decentralized administration that was not stuck in the old system and it was completely devoted to its task of privatising Russia. The more time that has passed, the more apparent it has become that this was a wise decision. As a concession to the old Soviet mentality, the regions were given plan indicators on privatisation.

All experience suggested that it was important to transform state enterprises into ordinary corporations and that it would not be possible to find able outsiders to put on corporate boards at an early stage. This was done in Russia. In Poland, large-scale privatization had been stalled, because the privatization law of July 1990 permitted several different groups of insiders to veto a privatization. Czechoslovakia had avoided this, instead encouraging the managers to take initiative, by demanding that they chose between about ten forms of privatization. Russia followed the Czechoslovak line, but limited the options to three, in practice two. In order both to break the political resistance of state managers and to speed up privatization, the Russian government from the very beginning tried to co-opt them through substantial cheap buy-outs by managers and employees, but the government was adamant that shares should be individual and not collective.

The distribution of vouchers was made as simple and sensible as possible. It was primarily inspired by Czechoslovakia. Everyone was given one voucher of equal value, but unlike in Czechoslovakia, even children received vouchers. As in Czechoslovakia, a small administrative fee was charged, so that it could not be argued that the state had paid in order to give its property away, which had been a damaging argument in Poland. People had to go to the post office and fetch the vouchers themselves, which meant that they had to show some initiative, at the same time the risk of fraud diminished. In contrast to Czechoslovakia, vouchers were transferable and tradable. The intention was both to give rise to a capital market and that people should realize the value of the vouchers, but their prices have stayed below the nominal level of 10,000 rubles.

While the Czechoslovak principle of voucher auctions was adopted in Russia, Czechoslovak centralized computer auctions were considered both too complex and too easily subject to fraud. Russia decided to focus upon decentralized, regional and simplified auctions. This led to popular involvement and a maximum of transparency. Exactly as in Czechoslovakia, people were allowed to bid directly at a voucher auction or by investing their vouchers with an investment fund. Again as in Czechoslovakia, anyone could organize a private investment fund, because in both countries leaders had learnt from the Polish failure to organize a few investment funds set up by the state. But because of a greater frequency of fraud, it was deemed necessary to license the investment funds in Russia.

A major difference from Poland was that privatization was led by one Minister (Anatoly Chubais) from November 1991. He took the initiative early on, acting as fast as was feasible, and he stuck stubbornly to one and the same privatization strategy. At the same time, he deftly showed the necessary flexibility to accomplish compromises with state mangers, workers and many regional leaders, while avoiding the old central state administration. In June 1992, he even succeeded in getting his key privatization legislation through the recalcitrant parliament, though this might have been equally a consequence of tenacity and luck. The emphasis lay on getting privatization done and accomplishing clear property rights and widespread ownership, while fair distribution was less emphasized.

The Russian large-scale privatization is a fine example of how East European experiences can be absorbed and exploited. Typically, the Russian policy-makers have not only asked what has been done, but also what has worked well and what has failed. Even when something has worked well in Czechoslovakia, the Russians have asked themselves whether the same model could work under Russian conditions. The Russian peculiarities upon which they have focused are: the poor functioning of the central state apparatus, the amount of fraud and corruption, and the weight of state managers and employees. In all, this amounts to a fine intellectual achievement, clarifying how useful East European experiences can be, if rightly understood. It is also a display of political skill.

## Has Poland been relevant as a model?

From our discussion above, it is rather easy to identify the major hurdles in the Russian change of economic system to date, and we shall relate each of them to the Polish experience.

The first obvious shortcoming in the Russian transformation is that the period of extraordinary politics was not exploited to a greater extent. It is impressive that price liberalization went as far as it did and that an attempt was made to achieve a relatively balanced budget, but a price liberalization for energy appeared possible but was not attempted. The Russian reform package was not as comprehensive as in Poland, and in this sense Russia failed to follow the Polish lead.

The second, more important mistake was not calling for parliamentary elections soon after the abortive coup in August 1991. The parliament became ever more troublesome and hostile to systemic change. In addition, it altered the constitution at its whim. In this regard, Russia made the same mistake as Poland had. Moreover, economists in both countries, as well as in the West, tend to look upon elections as time-consuming complications, while parliamentary elections were a necessary precondition for breaking the power of the old elite and the industrial lobbies in Russia. In Poland, it turned out to be possible to check their power by other means. Therefore, the Polish experience led in the wrong direction as it was interpreted. As the preconditions in Russia were more difficult, this misinterpretation became more costly in Russia than in Poland. The conclusion is that appropriate political advice was missing in both countries.

Third, there is a striking difference in Russia between the success of large-scale privatization carried out by a new administration and the relative failure of stabilization poorly pursued by the old bureaucracy as well as the outright sabotages of liberalization by the Ministry of the Economy under Oleg Lobov and the State Price Committee. The important lesson is that unlike Poland, Russia needed to build a new policy-making apparatus because the old administration was too deeply set in its old ideas and practices, without the will or ability to adjust. Still, considering the problems Poland had experienced with its old bureaucracy, the larger size of Russia and the restive nature of the administration, it would be a logical conclusion to draw from the Polish experience.

Fourth, Poland had proved that a swift, far-reaching domestic and external liberalization and a strict macroeconomic stabilization were a successful path. The problems in Russia exemplify how important it is to go sufficiently far in all these directions. On the one hand, Poland showed the way. On the other hand, since Poland had succeeded, it did not illuminate how costly it would be to fail. The Polish experiences did not clarify how important it was to move sufficiently far and fast or how much it would cost a country like Russia not to move swiftly enough, but the experiences of one single country could never provide a sufficient answer to this question. The obvious conclusion is that the more messy the situation is, the more important it is to go for a rigorous solution with a maximum of liberalization and stabilization.

Fifth, in hindsight it is evident that the earlier the ruble zone had been broken up, the better it would have been for all concerned. The countries that benefited from Russian subsidies appear to have wasted more by not going for a swift change of economic system. Here, the Czechoslovak experience of 1919 provides the best lesson, and neither Poland nor any other current example would have been of much use.

Sixth, Poland provided the whole range of arguments and experiments in the sphere of privatization. Thus, Russia could learn from Poland's intellectual endeavours and practical failures, avoiding the same pitfalls itself. For instance, privatization could only be carried out effectively at a regional level. Poland had drawn the same lesson in its small-scale privatization, and the Russian privatisers drew the right conclusion from the Polish and Czechoslovak experiences, given that Russia is a much bigger country and has an administration that functions very inefficiently.

Seventh, both Poland and Russia illustrate the importance of coordinated Western financial action, but the big difference is that Russia did not enjoy access to financial support when it was ready. Hopefully, a new round of economic stabilization will lead to better coordination between Russian liberalization and stabilization, on the one hand, and Western financing, on the other.

Finally, it is fair to raise the question of whether the political forces against stabilization and liberalization were so strong in Russia that it would not have been possible to undermine them without prior privatization. Such a conclusion could have far-reaching repercussions, but even so it is difficult to suggest any alternative sequencing. Essentially, this means that the first attempt at stabilization is likely to fail, while the second one enjoys a much greater chance of success, because many members of the old elite have adjusted and jumped upon the reform bandwagon, when they realized that they can do even better in that fashion.

A major conclusion from this comparison is that the differences in political preconditions have been of crucial importance. Unfortunately, economists tend to overlook such facts and assume that the state does function. On the contrary, the post-communist states function extremely badly (Åslund, 1992). The most important difference between Poland and Russia turns out to be that the Russian state administration functions much worse. It is all too evident that a thorough political handling of the old elite was far more important in Russia than in Poland, while in fact even less was initially done in Russia. This is the outstanding mistake in Russia, and the main means should have been democratic elections both to parliament and to regional authorities. In addition, there is a strong argument for a maximal reduction of the central state administration, since much of this administration worked full-time on sabotaging both the design and execution of the government's policy.

Another significant precondition is the degree of acute financial crises at the outset of reforms. The consequences of differing economic structures between Poland and Russia are not evident as yet, if we leave aside the political balance, in which the political weight of industrial lobbies was much heavier in Russia. A reasonable suggestion is that the greater the distortions are, the more difficult it will be to transform society. Therefore, it is both more important and more difficult to take a truly radical approach in a society more deeply ingrained in socialism. Therefore, the worse off a society is to begin with, the more costly the transition is likely to be, which corresponds to the experiences to date (Åslund, 1992).

At present, it is popular to suggest that Russia should have turned to the Chinese strategy of gradual reform instead (Chen, Jeffersson and Singh, 1992; McKinnon, 1993). However, our scrutiny of the problems with the application in Russia of Polish lessons suggests that the Chinese experiences would not have provided relevant answers to any of the major problems that we have pinpointed, and only a few of the minor ones, such as the importance of using the regional administration and the realization that tax revenues would fall as a share of GDP with liberalization. Such articles tend to conclude with recommendations for Russia to adopt more gradualist policies, including more price regulations and restrictions on trade. But as we have shown above, Russia has been too gradualist. Thus, the very prescriptions of these articles show that China is not relevant as an example (Åslund, 1989). This is all the more evident in the case of relatively well-functioning states such as Germany, Japan, South Korea, Singapore and Taiwan. To refer to them as examples for Russia is primarily evidence of disregard for essential preconditions and the most fundamental peculiarity of Russia, namely the weakness of the state.

The current Russian discussion shows an interesting trend. A number of young intellectuals propose ever more liberal schemes, realizing how poorly the state is functioning (Vasiliev, 1993; Lvin, 1992; Naishul, 1992). Friedrich Hayek constitutes the mainstream in this thinking. This line of argument appears a rational reaction to a realization of the moral bankruptcy of the Russian state administration.

In comparison, Poland appears to have been the most relevant example at hand. The shortcomings of the Russian transformation may be subdivided into three groups: 1) failure to do what Poland did, 2) failure to realize the necessary political underpinnings of shock therapy, and 3) worse conditions due to a weaker state, less Western attention, and the breaking up of the Soviet Union. Thus, the Russian reformers are to be congratulated that they were wise enough to turn to the Polish model in spite of massive criticism.

## Notes

* Much of this paper is based on discussions with Jeffrey Sachs, Marek Dabrowski, Jacek Rostowski, David Lipton and Andrew Berg.

1. Notably, Jeffrey Sachs, Marek Dabrowski, Jacek Rostowski and David Lipton.
2. Dabrowski (1993a) has undertaken a similar study, but his emphasis lay on what lessons Russia can draw from Poland's experience.
3. In Poland Wladyslaw Baka was a professor of economics and a former Deputy Prime Minister for economic reform; in Russia, it was the long-time head of the Soviet state bank, Viktor Gerashchenko.
4. *Rossiiskaya gazeta*, 22 May 1993, p. 1.

## References

Åslund, Anders (1989) "Soviet and Chinese Reforms – Why They Must Be Different", *The World Today*, vol. 14, no. 11, pp. 188-191.

Åslund, Anders (1991) *Gorbachev's Struggle for Economic Reform,* 2nd ed., Pinter, London.

— (1992) *The Post-Communist Economic Revolution: How Big a Bang?,* Center for Strategic and International Studies, Washington, DC.

— (1993) "The Gradual Nature of Economic Change in Russia" in Åslund and Layard, pp. 19-38.

Åslund, Anders, and Richard Layard, eds. (1993) *Changing the Economic System in Russia,* Pinter, London.

Balcerowicz, Leszek (1992) *800 dni. Szok kontrolowany*, BGW, Warsaw.

Bogomolov, Oleg (1992) "Net ni vremeni, ni effektivnoi vlasti", *Nezavisimaya gazeta,* 7 February, p. 4.

Boycko, Maxim, and Andrei Shleifer (1993) "The Voucher Program for Russia" in Åslund and Layard, pp. 100-111.

Chen, Kang, Gary H. Jeffersson and Inderjit Singh (1992) "Lessons from China's Economic Reform", *Journal of Comparative Economics*, vol. 16, pp. 201-225.

Chubais, Anatoly B., and Maria Vishnevskaya (1993) "Main Issues of Privatization in Russia" in Åslund and Layard, pp. 89-99.

Dabrowski, Marek (1993a) "The First Half Year of Russian Transformation" in Åslund and Layard, pp. 1-18.

— (1993b) "From Soviet Rouble to National Roubles. Evolution of the Rouble Area in 1991-1992", Paper presented at the Third Trento Workshop on Integration and Disintegration in European Economies.

Frydman, Roman, Andrzej Rapaczynski, John S. Earle, et al (1993) *The Privatization Process in Central Europe,* Central European University Press, Budapest, London and New York.

Government of Russian Federation (1992) *Russian Economic Trends*, vol. 1, nos. 1-3.

Gros, Daniel (1992) "Inter-State Economic Relations in the Former Soviet Union", *CEPS Working Document* no. 63.

Hansson, Ardo H. (1993a) "The Trouble with the Ruble: Monetary Reform in the Former Soviet Union" in Åslund and Layard, pp. 163-182.

Hansson, Ardo H. (1993b) "The Baltic States: Differences Begin to Emerge", *Östekonomisk Rapport,* vol. 5, no. 4.

Hawrylyshyn, Oleh, and John Williamson (1991) *From Soviet disUnion to Eastern Economic Community?* Institute for International Economics, Washington, DC.

Lipton, David, and Jeffrey Sachs (1992) "Prospects for Russia's Economic Reforms", *Brookings Papers on Economic Activity,* no. 2, pp. 213-283.

Lvin, Boris (1992) "Kak delat' revolyutsiyu. Neskol'ko sovetov pravitelstvu Rossii", *Nezavisimaya gazeta*, 10 March, p. 5.

Major, Ivan (1993) *Privatisation in Eastern Europe*, Elgar.

McKinnon, Ronald I. (1993) "Gradual versus Rapid Liberalization in Socialist Economies: Financial Policies and Macroeconomic Stability in China and Russia Compared", Paper presented at the Annual World Bank Conference on Development Economics, 3-4 May.

Naishul, Vitaly (1992) "Perspektivy liberal'nykh reform", *Nezavisimaya gazeta*, 21 October, p. 4.

Pasvolsky, L. (1928) *Economic Nationalism of the Danubian States*, Macmillan, New York.

"Platezhnyi balans RF za 1992 god" (1993) *Ekonomicheskaya gazeta*, no. 18, May, p. 5.

Rostowski, Jacek (1993) "The Inter-enterprise Debt Explosion in the Former Soviet Union: Causes, Consequences, Cures", *Communist Economies and Economic Transformation*, vol. 5, no. 2, pp. 131-159.

Sachs, Jeffrey (1993) "Achieving Monetary Stabilization in Russia in 1993", mimeo., 7 March.

Sachs, Jeffrey, and David Lipton (1993) "Remaining Steps to Achieve a Market-Based Monetary System" in Åslund and Layard, pp. 127-162.

Sargent, Thomas J. (1986) *Rational Expectations and Inflation*, Harper & Row, New York.

Tsentralnyi Bank Rossiiskoi Federatsii (1992) "O stabilizatsii denezhno-kreditnoi sistemy", *Voprosy ekonomiki*, no. 12, pp. 4-22.

Vasiliev, Sergei (1993) "Economic Reform in Russia: Social, Political, and Institutional Aspects" in Åslund and Layard, pp. 72-86.

Yeltsin, Boris N. (1991) "Vystuplenie B. N. Yel'tsina", *Sovetskaya Rossiya*, 29 October, pp. 1 and 3.

# 11 Economic Reforms: A Liberal Perspective

*Vitaly Naishul* *

## Introduction

Russia is going through another difficult period. The current reforms, which started with great risks and hopes, have only partially justified the aspirations. On the one hand, the population as a whole has adapted to the new economic situation rather smoothly and has not protested against the reforms. In fact from February to May 1992, it seems that the population began to show growing respect for the authorities, in spite of the current weakness of the state. On the other hand, few opportunities have opened in the economy now, at least in comparison with market-oriented expectations.

After making a first decisive move toward liberalizing the economy, the government suddenly halted. Since then, the foremost deeds of the government have been introducing mass privatization by voucher and liberalizing energy prices. However, it is doubtful that these reforms will bring substantially more economic freedom to society. Administrative methods are still applied to current economic problems.

Through the liberalization of prices, the government has sharply strengthened the role of finance, which is a centralized lever of economic policy. In addition to the economic and political pressures from different groups, government bodies are guided by their own assessment of the efficiency of different industries or by their own self-interest. Thus they began to use financial leverage, as well as privileges and licenses, with the same arbitrariness and ease as Brezhnev's ministries displayed when they allocated physical resources. As a result of this policy, the severity, but equity, of the new economic relations has not been understood by society.

After *Perestroika* and *Liberalization*, as Yelena Bonner has put it, a period of

*Democratic stagnation* has begun. The unresolved problems are intensifying public tensions and a worsening political situation. Deprived of the tutelage of the paternal state, people feel this tension because they are still fettered by the rudiments of the old system, giving them little opportunity to care for themselves.

The government has made at least two substantial mistakes that have brought about the crises. First, it tried to implement a monetary system alien to the national economy of Russia. Second, the state sector was not forced to accommodate to the liberalization, and the rigidities of the state enterprises broke the intended tight monetary policy.

Anyone familiar with the activities of the planning agencies knows how great an effort was exerted on the distribution of each product; how difficult it was to reject the request of someone in need or a friend who has helped you; how many officials were eager to be bribed; and even how commodities not produced were often distributed. People had no illusions about how things would work. It was easy to predict the behavior of state bodies that were issuing and distributing money, a commodity which did not take much effort or expense to produce. The examples of other countries with a weak central banking system and a weak state have adequately shown the inefficiency of having a central bank that is supposed to observe abstract monetary interests.

Another major problem is that the stabilization measures did not take into account the variety of exchange relations which existed before the reforms. Exchange relations were always monetarized in retail trade and among the population. Therefore, they responded adequately to the monetary policy. Between enterprises, however, other non-monetarized types of exchange relations prevailed, and there the monetary policy caused massive inter-enterprise arrears.

Tough monetary policy, which the government failed to introduce, has the same kind of relationship to liberalism as tough planning policy. The liberal approach regards money as a commodity that promotes current exchanges and future transactions, and suggests methods, such as the opening of currency markets and free competition between all means of exchange, ranging from tires to rubles and dollars.

The Russian government has tried to introduce a tough financial policy, while preserving the hierarchical bureaucratic framework and the old socialist regulations. Except for deregulating retail trade on the street, as in Poland, the government did not take any steps toward seriously liberalizing production and trade. Analyzing the Gaidar government's actions, we see that it became a major source of economic restrictions. Many of the government's measures, such as heavy taxation, rendered the economy even less flexible, by driving business activities to the black market, thus hampering the formation of legal market institutions.

## Prerequisites of a liberal economic policy

### *Withering of the state*

The aim of the former system of economic management was to eradicate trade and substitute for it scientifically stipulated administrative distribution. However, the system turned out to be applicable only under specific external conditions. The substantial changes in these conditions in the 1950s led to the spontaneous transformation of the administrative command system into an administrative or bureaucratic market. As a result, the trade which had been eliminated outside the state sector started to develop within it.

The flourishing of administrative trade allowed administrative bodies to rapidly form autonomous economic rights. This phenomenon was called *vedomstvenost'* or *departmentalism*.

The decline of government power, which was intensified by perestroika and especially by the withdrawal of the Communist Party as an integrator of all power structures, made the state bodies even more autonomous, and gave them increased freedom to develop supplementary business activities and sources of revenue. To a great extent, bureaucratic trade was replaced by barter and regular trade. Former state departments transformed themselves into commercial agencies, pursuing their own economic interests.

Thus, Russia is now facing two inter-connected tasks: to complete the process of *commercialization of state agencies* by removing them from their bureaucratic framework (separating the economy from the state), and to *establish an effective non-trading state* which will be able to protect private property and contractual rights (separating the state from the economy).

### *Structural policy*

According to many scholars, and primarily the school of Dr. Y. V. Yaremenko, Russia's economy is full of structural disproportion and is far from the homogeneity which is ideal for an efficient functioning of a market economy. Two different practical conclusions can be drawn from this observation: a traditional-structural solution or a liberal one.

Traditionalists find it expedient to divide the economy into several more or less homogeneous sectors and to establish a specific set of game rules for each sector, including: taxation, exchange rates, privileges, etc. This solution requires that the state has enough organizational potential to draw borders between them, and to maintain control over these borders. From a liberal perspective, the free market leaves enough room for structural variety, and moreover, the problems of structural disproportion are short-lived and can be solved efficiently, if they are not entrenched by state regulations that restrict economic activities.

An example from current economic policy can illustrate this point. At the beginning of 1992, a large gap existed in Russia between the value of cash and non-cash, or accounting, rubles; the informal exchange rate was 2:1. In the past, the structuralist approach was exercised, with tough control over exchange. According to the liberal view, it would be beneficial to allow a free exchange rate between these two types of rubles. In practice, structural disproportion such as this gap were simply ignored by the government, that established the highly artificial exchange rate of 1:1, which caused a cash shortage in the beginning, and surplus of money thereafter.

The modern Russian state is weak, in fact it is practically absent, allowing laws to be traded, and this makes it impossible to exercise a structuralist policy. Under the pretext of exercising structural economic policy, I would expect a corrupt and unfair distribution of privileges to the strongest, and the suppression of the weakest. Thus, the profound liberalization of economic activities is an essential premise for the survival of the economy.

### *The composition of society*

There are two major factors that make a liberal solution feasible for Russia. First, the essential requirement for the administrative system to function effectively was the standardization and uniformity of the objects of management. Over the 50-year history of the administrative system, a high degree of societal homogeneity has been achieved. In Dr Boris M. Lvin's view, this eliminates the danger of serious conflicts and is a prerequisite to the formation of a liberal society.

Second, the long-term prohibition of independent activities has intensified the development of informal ties, practically hidden from state interference. The existence of an informal non-state network, which satisfies the majority of human demands, makes the society capable of organizing itself and preserving stability while the state withers away. This means that state control can be withdrawn from most spheres of society without risk for the destablization of the country.

In the current system, the central authorities can influence spontaneous reforms, by depriving the old bureaucratic relations of legitimacy, thus liberalizing the economy. The central government is too weak to build a new state, much less a new society. However, it has the right to legitimize the state hierarchical relations and can therefore shape the development of a new state system.

## Liberal reform

### *Institutional liberalization*

The first step of liberal reform made by the government was the liberalization of prices. This meant the de facto termination of the legal support of central authorities to the previous mutual obligations between the population and the retail trade of the state and enterprises, with regard to the regulation of prices and the remuneration of labor. Now it is necessary to complete this process by liberalizing the relations between organizations. This means terminating the central authorities' support of mutual bureaucratic claims on state departments and enterprises.

This policy may be characterized as *institutional liberalization*. The central government can proclaim that it will no longer support the subordination of all the former state departments, except for an explicitly stipulated list of them. Institutional liberalization is the logical conclusion and the final step in the decades-long process of liberalizing the state departments. The process of market-oriented reforms in the Russian economy will not be completed until this step is taken.

Indeed, institutional liberalization means the total privatization of practically all the former pseudo-state property. After this step, only local inter-group struggles for the redistribution of property can emerge. Most of these conflicts will be settled informally. Only in rare cases will court intervention be necessary in order to divide common property on the basis of customary law and existing legal norms.

Institutional liberalization also means total deregulation, because it presumes the termination of subordination to almost all the former state regulatory offices. Institutional liberalization could make the economy even more liquid, if it could be extended to revenue services and compulsory taxation could be abolished. This option will be discussed in short below.

### *Limits of the state*

What should be the functions of the *New Russian State*? As world experience shows, practically all public goods, such as communications, education, medical services and even the monetary system, can be efficiently privatized. The spontaneous processes in our country are going in this very direction.

However, if citizens want to have lasting internal peace there is one function which cannot be alienated from the state. The state must guarantee that whenever a conflict in society cannot be settled on the basis of mutual agreements, the state will resolve it with enough force so that it cannot be disputed by non-state physical or legal persons.

In most cases, non-state institutions can be used to execute the decisions of the state. A criminal investigation may be carried out by private agencies, and private security agencies can arrest culprits and maintain order in the streets. The latter is already taking place today.

This change in the role of the state and the loss of its former economic functions may transform state officials from "operational managers" into "impartial" and "incorruptible" persons. Patriotic efforts should be aimed at creating such a state. The state also has the function of protecting citizens from threats from abroad, and pursuing relevant foreign policy.

### *Privatization of the state debt*

Institutional liberalization will take away nearly all assets from the state. Then the remaining state debts will place a heavy tax burden on the budding market economy. Moreover, even greater potential earnings will be lost as a result of the tough control exercised by tax authorities in order to collect huge revenues. The state's debt in terms of pensions to older citizens is the single biggest state liability. By our estimate, amounts to more than $500 bn at world prices, and greatly exceeds Russia's debt. The pension debt can be efficiently privatized by transferring both rights and pension liabilities (in the form of annuities) to local private funds. our opinion, it is possible to work out ways of privatizing the other state debts too. The privatization of state liabilities appears to be the main economic problem of the privatization process, but even so, insufficient attention is devoted to it.

### *Taxation*

By privatizing state debts, withdrawing the state from the economy and reforming the military, state expenditures would drop sharply to several percent of GNP. This extremely low level of state expenditures, and therefore low taxation, will make tax evasion more costly than simply paying taxes. This will allow tax control over enterprises to be less severe and harmful. The authors of this paper are currently elaborating an idea for extending institutional liberalization to taxation, thus abolishing compulsory taxes. This would facilitate the opening of markets and promote increased economic freedom. The idea is to find a social mechanism to encourage a sufficient number of Russian citizens to finance the minimal state expenditures.

### *Monetary system*

One of the main results of institutional liberalization will be changes in the monetary system, which in practice will mean the following:

1. The Central Bank of Russia will be the only commercial bank with its own banknotes denominated in rubles of current issue. Rubles of the Central Bank of Russia will compete with foreign currency and probably with banknotes of other commercial banks.
2. Each commercial bank will be able to quote the deposit money of other banks so that excessive emission will be punished by a falling exchange rate.
3. Banking in Russia will be opened to foreign banks which can bring in modern banking technology and standards of credibility and services.

As a result, Russia will have a free banking system with competitive currencies, analogous to the system which existed in Western countries before centralized banking developed. In this system, there will be no state body responsible for the amount of money in circulation, and thus no inflation, which has proven inevitable in other cases.

## Note

* This paper was originally prepared by the Institute for the Study of The Russian Economy, and presented at a seminar of the Centre for Economic Reforms of the Russian Government held 10-11 October 1992. The paper was written by Vitali Naishul, and prepared by V. V. Agroskin, V. F. Chesnokova, V. L. Kagansky, S. G. Kordonsky, G. V. Lebedev, A. I. Levenchuk, B. M. Lvin, V. A. Naishul, S. Yu. Pavlenko and G. G. Sapov. A prior version was published in *Nezavisimaya gazeta*, October 22, 1992.

# Index

*Numerals and entries in boldface refer to a major section. In addition to the names and subject entries in this index, see also Notes at end of each chapter.*